MW00573681

A special thanks
to everyone
who has helped make
Know Yourself
what it is today.

Dear Reader

Knowing yourself is truly the beginning of all wisdom. We give young learners the building blocks they need to start their unique journey of self-discovery: an understanding of human anatomy — literally how we are put together. Knowledge of one's own human body is an empowering context on which anyone can build.

Learning about the body and mind at a young age sets the foundation for honoring one's physical form, develops self-esteem and self-confidence, and begins the discovery of who we are meant to be in this world.

Now that's real power.

The Know Yourself Team

Quick-Start Guide

Hello Know Yourselfers!

Follow these steps to start a new journey and explore the immune system. Have fun on this Self Literacy quest and remember - Keep your wits about you!

1

Grab an umbrella and a cup of tea! We are going to England.

Locate England on your atlas, or find an online map of the world.

2

Read Time Skaters Adventure 6.

Pinky and Bounski encounter the legendary King Arthur and his Knights. Camelot needs the Time Skaters!

3

Get equipped!

Suit up and gather your provisions listed on the inventory page. There are more battles to be won by you and the Immune Platoon!

Table of Contents

Hello Adventurer!

Welcome to Adventure 6 - The Immune System.

During this adventure, you will explore Arthurian England and your body's immune system. There will be information to read and activities to complete to help you learn, and quizzes when you are ready to challenge yourself! Take your time along the way - spend as much or as little time as you like on each activity, and do not forget to use the additional resources to learn more about the topics you are interested in.

My name is Dr. Bonyfide. I'm lost in the space-time continuum! Help my friends search for me, and learn about history and science along the way.

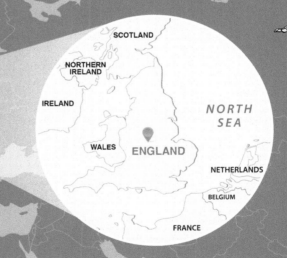

Wilcume!*

That means "Welcome!" in Old English.

*Say it like this: "wil-coom."
*Syllables in bold are the strongest.

LEARN ABOUT

The Immune System

Armed with a cellular battalion, your body protects itself from invasion.

VISIT

Arthurian England

In a mysterious mist, a kingdom fraught /
And a strange affliction caught /
With Merlin's help, our heroes sought /
How Germs are rid of on the spot!

MEET

King Arthur

The Knights of the Round Table, Merlin, and a few other extraordinary characters.

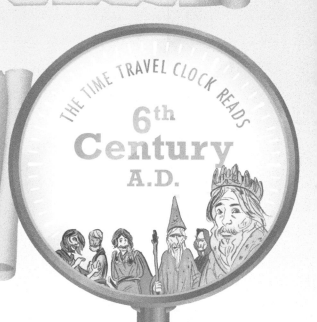

THE TIME TRAVEL CLOCK READS

6th **Century** A.D.

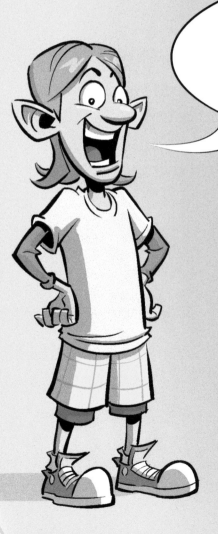

Enter
this portal

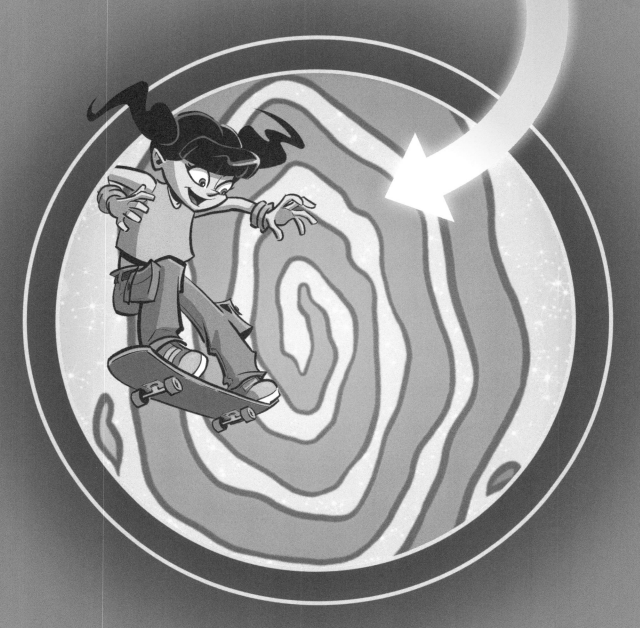

for
Time Skaters Adventure 6...

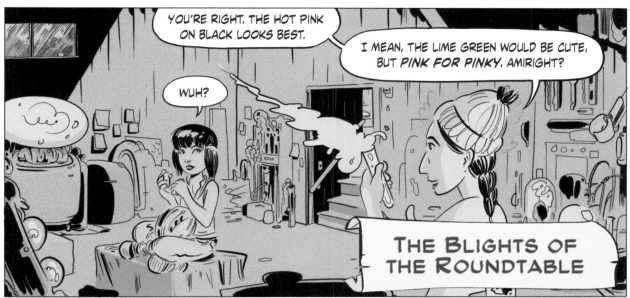

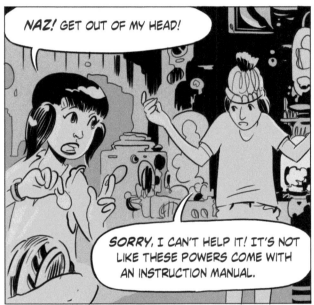

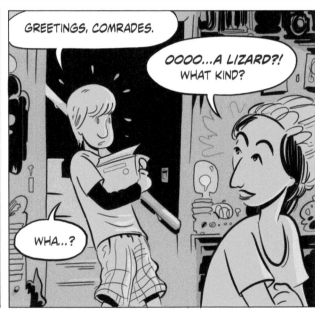

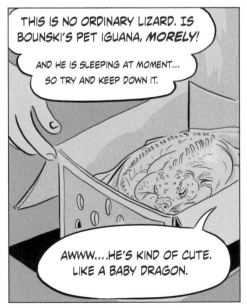

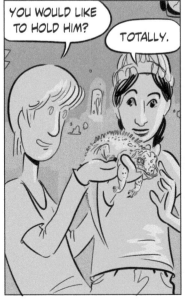

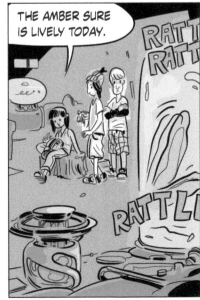

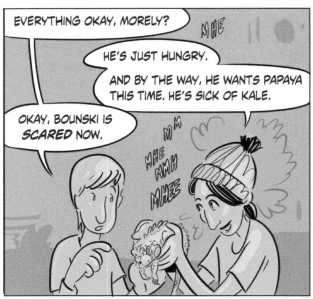

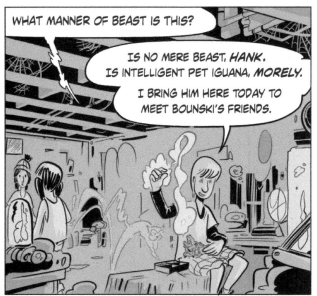

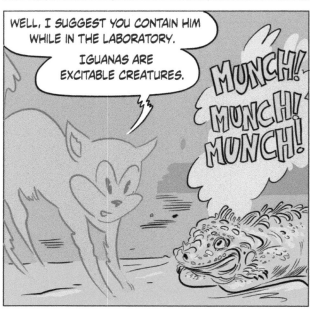

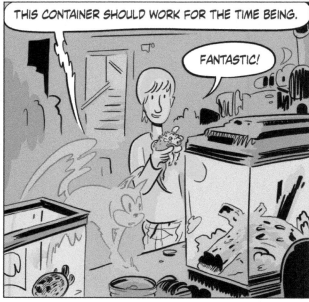

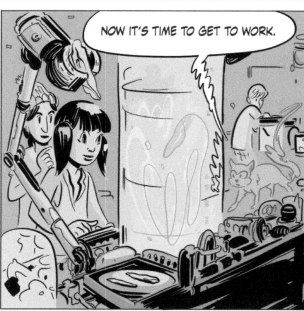

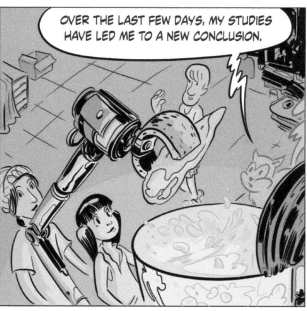

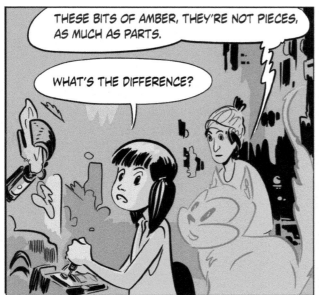

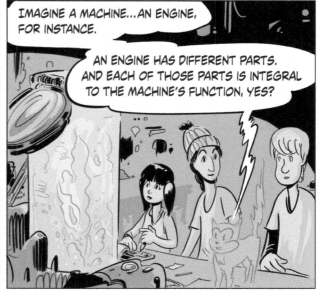

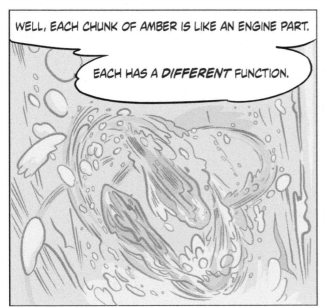

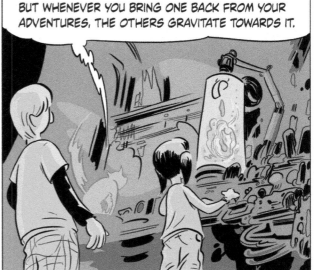

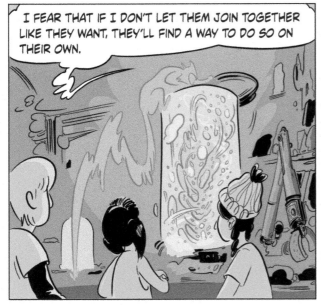

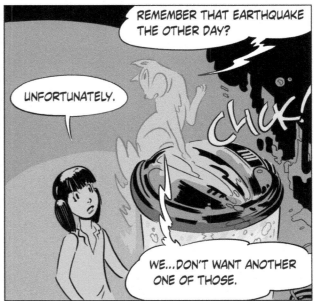

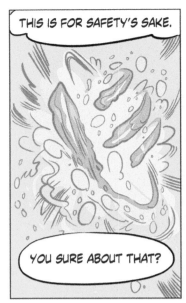

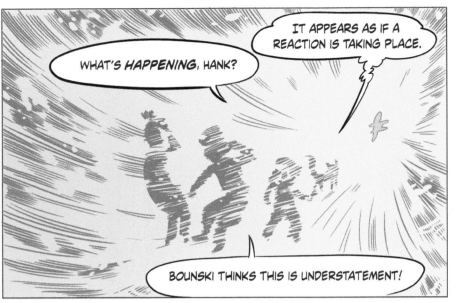

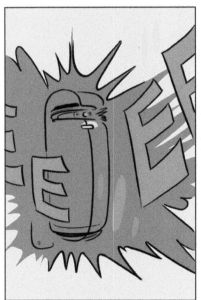

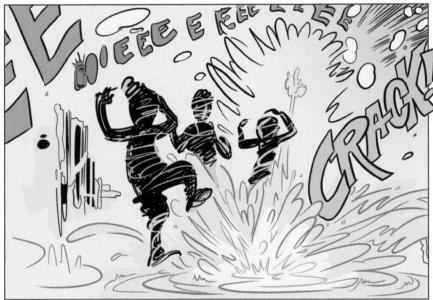

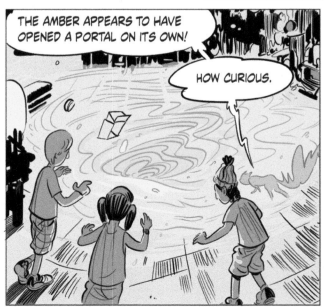

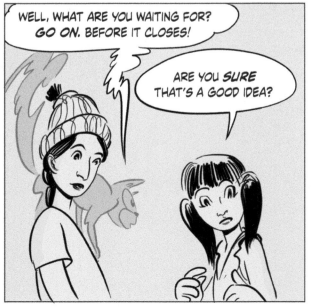

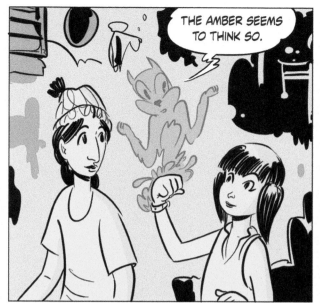
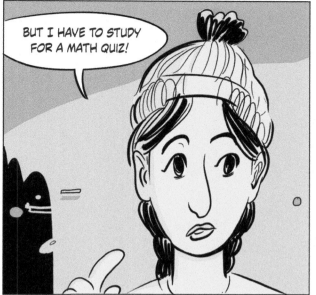
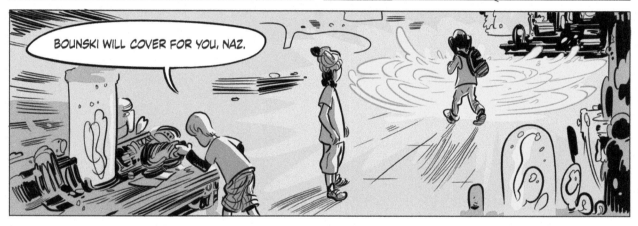
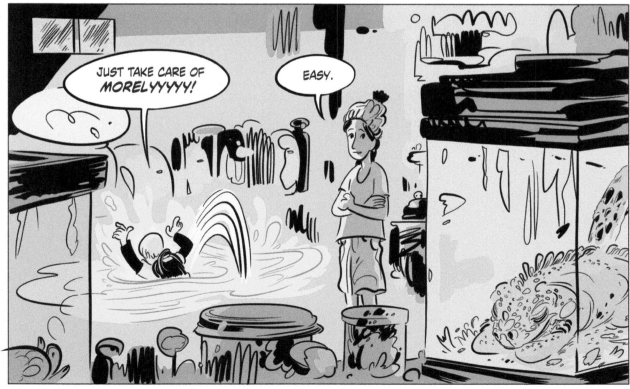

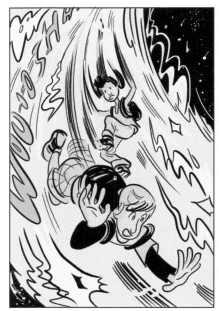

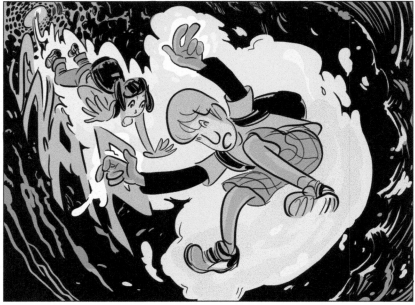

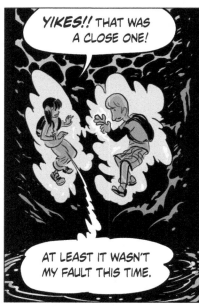

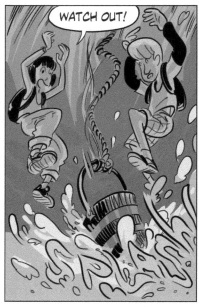

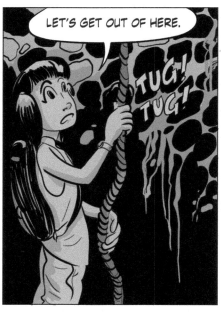

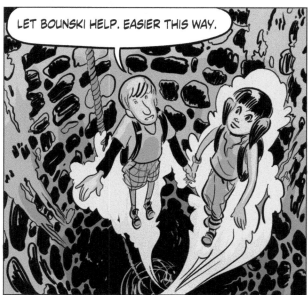

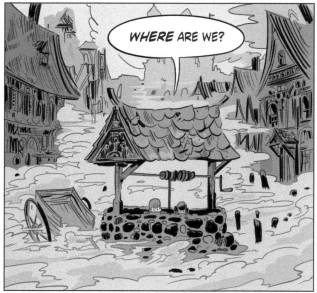

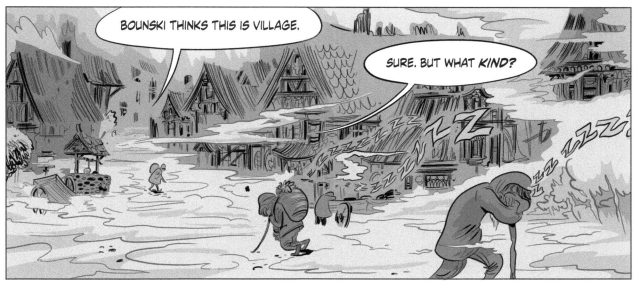

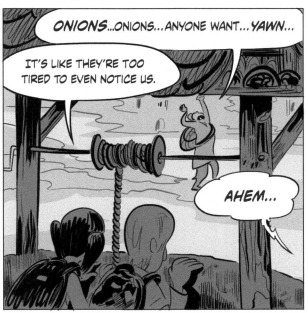

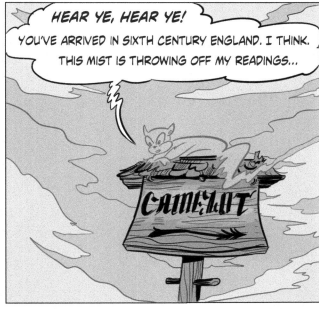

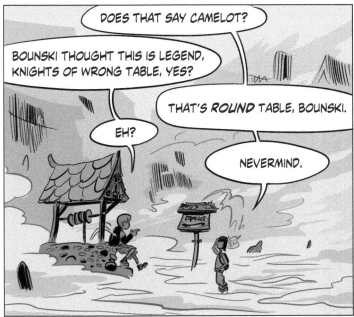

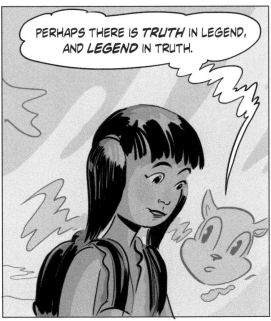

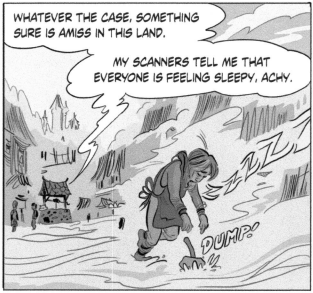

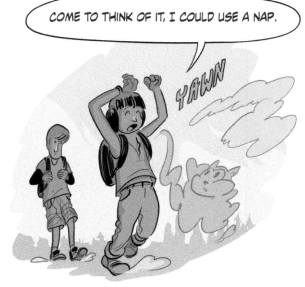

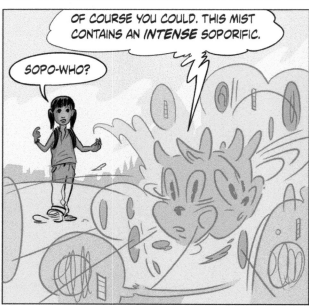

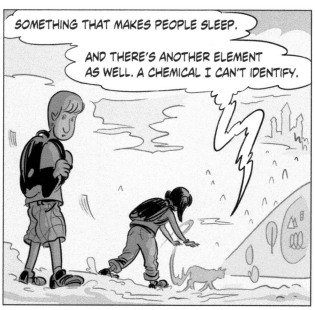

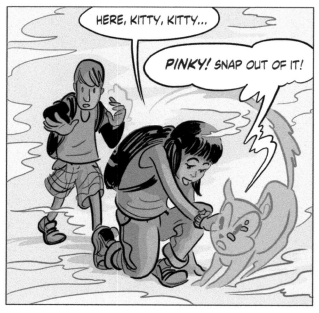

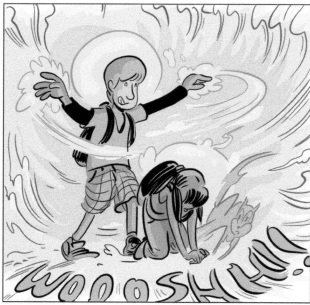

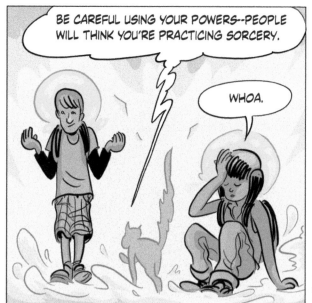

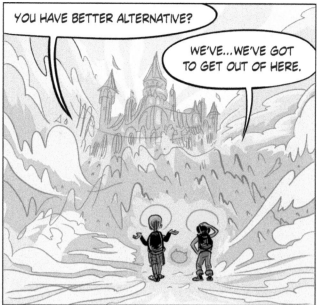

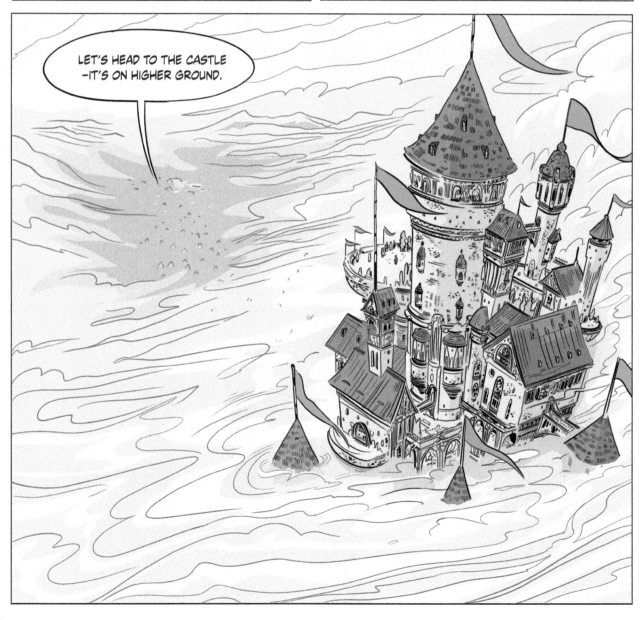

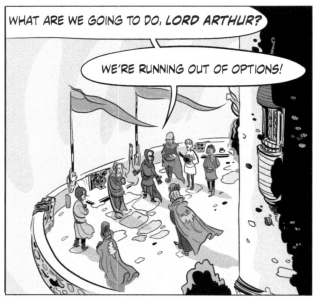

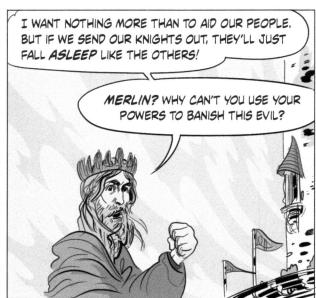

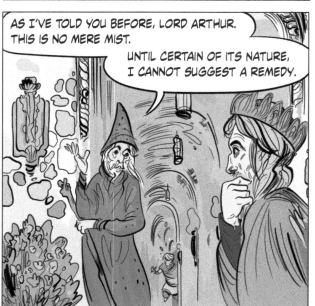

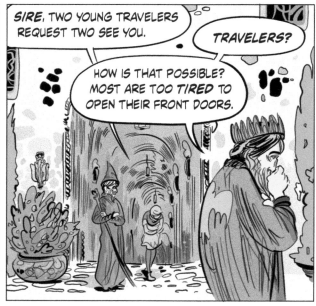

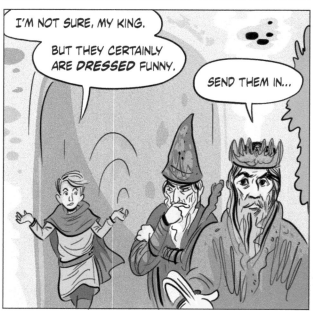

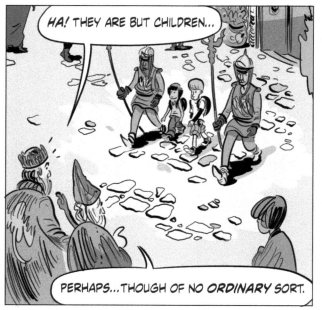

THE IMMUNE SYSTEM

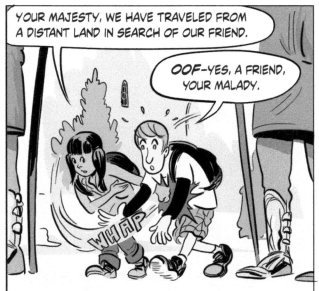

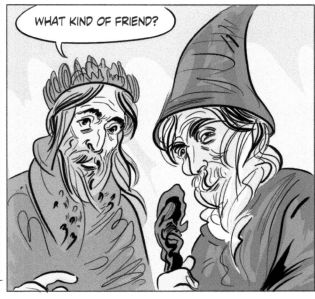

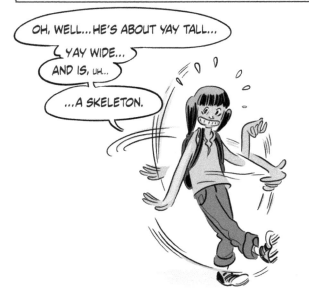

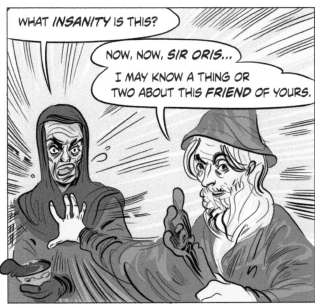

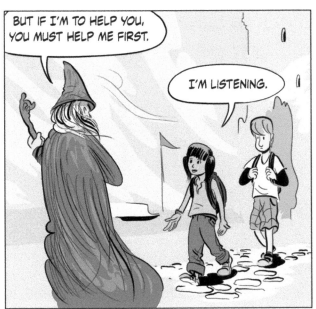

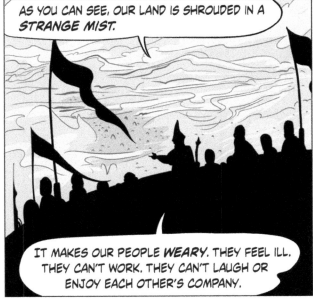

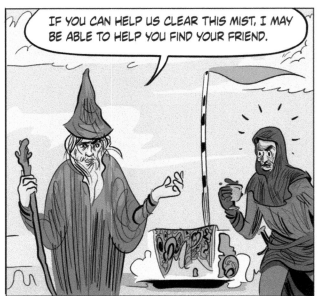

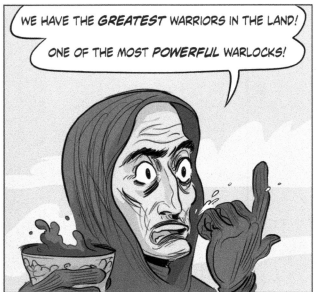

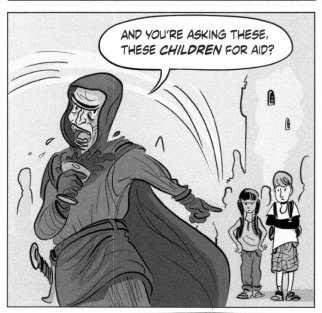

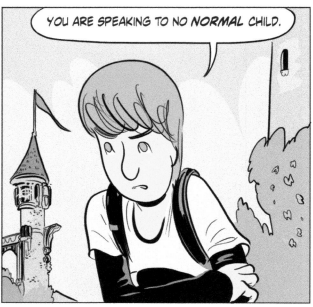

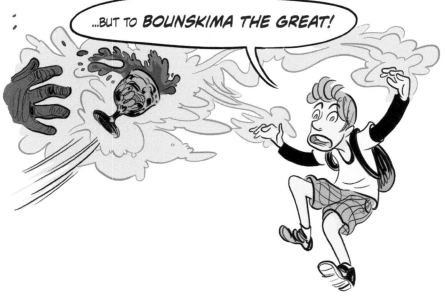

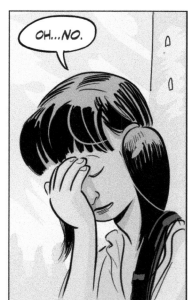

THE IMMUNE SYSTEM

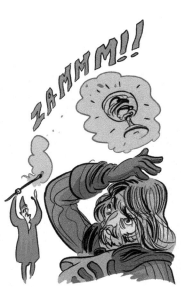

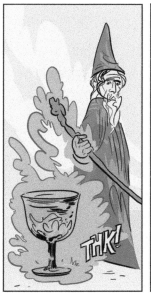

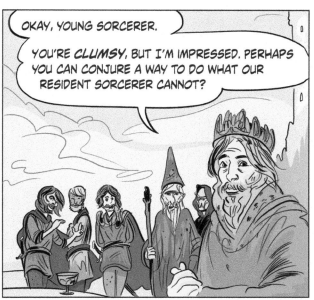

OKAY, YOUNG SORCERER.

YOU'RE *CLUMSY*, BUT I'M IMPRESSED. PERHAPS YOU CAN CONJURE A WAY TO DO WHAT OUR RESIDENT SORCERER CANNOT?

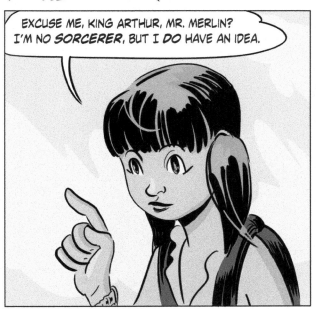

EXCUSE ME, KING ARTHUR, MR. MERLIN? I'M NO *SORCERER*, BUT I *DO* HAVE AN IDEA.

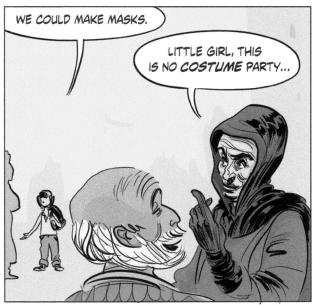

WE COULD MAKE MASKS.

LITTLE GIRL, THIS IS NO *COSTUME* PARTY...

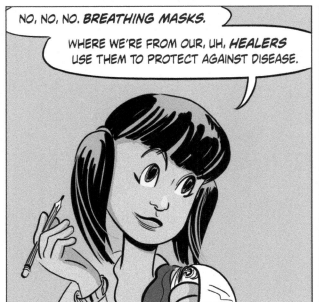

NO, NO, NO. *BREATHING MASKS.*

WHERE WE'RE FROM OUR, UH, *HEALERS* USE THEM TO PROTECT AGAINST DISEASE.

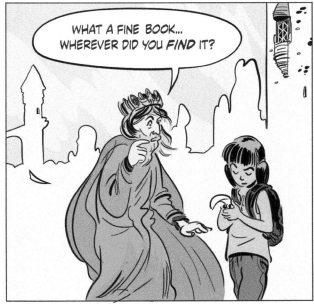

WHAT A FINE BOOK... WHEREVER DID YOU *FIND* IT?

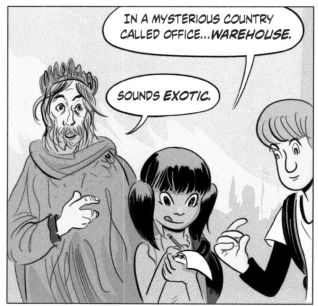
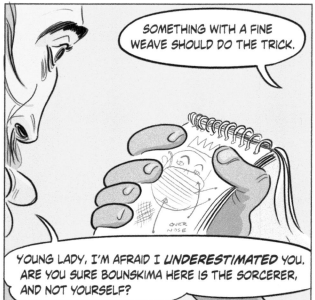
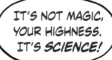
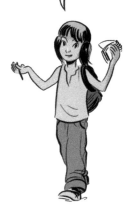
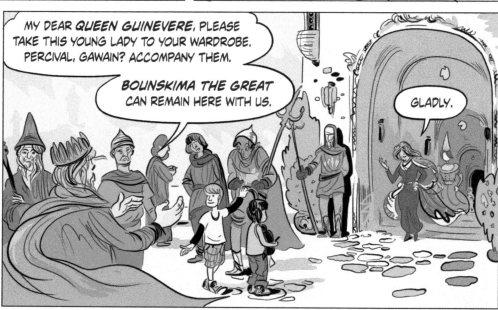
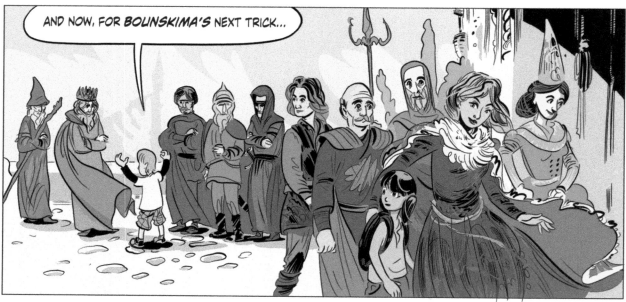

THE IMMUNE SYSTEM

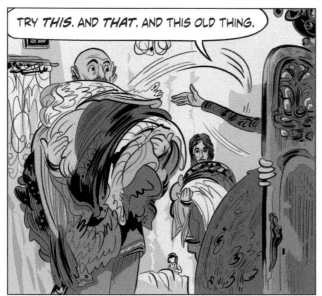

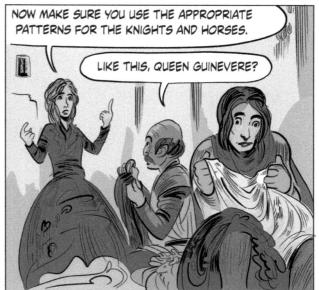

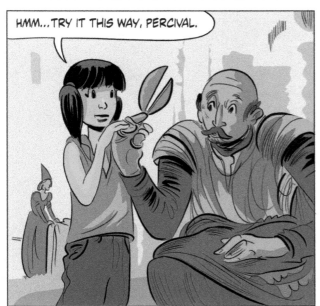

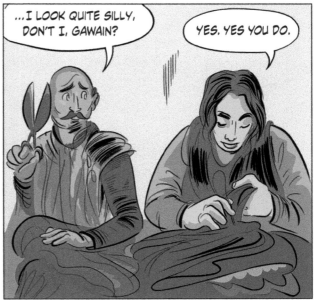

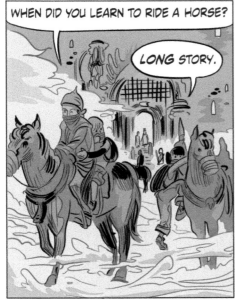

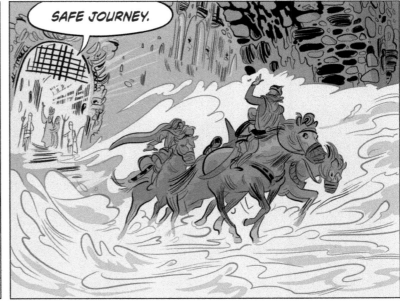

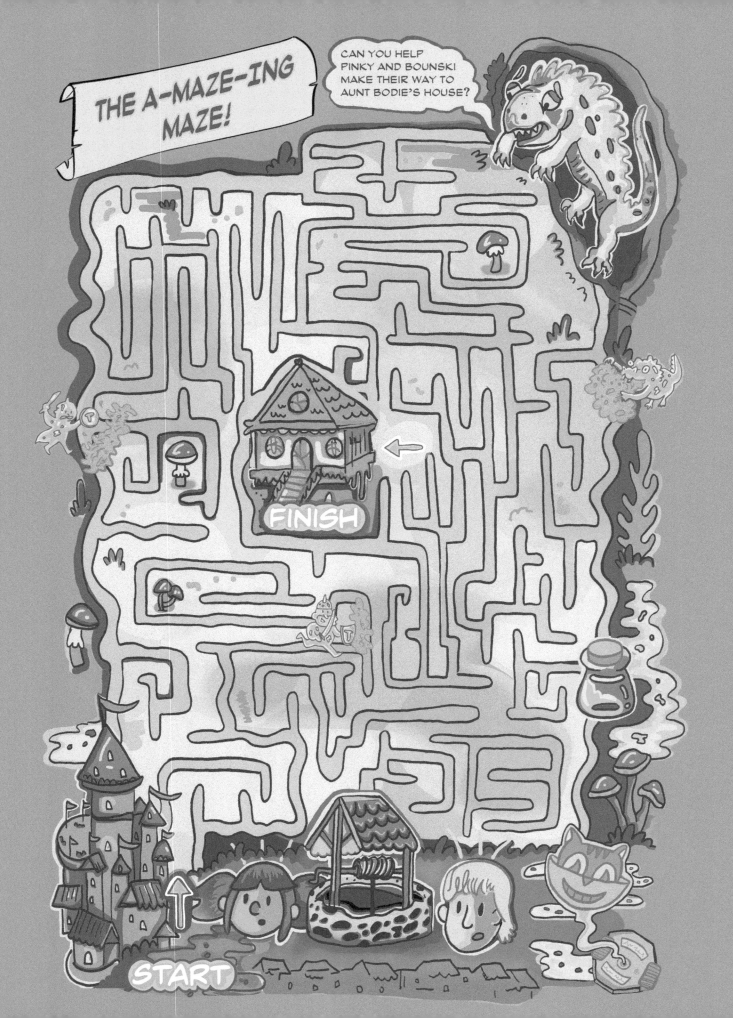

THE IMMUNE SYSTEM

You might have heard people talk about a 'stomach bug' or 'flu bug,' but germs aren't bugs at all. They're much smaller.

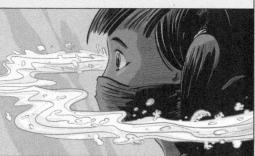

In fact, they're so **tiny** that you can't see them without a microscope. The word germ usually refers to a variety of **pathogens***, or things that can get you sick.

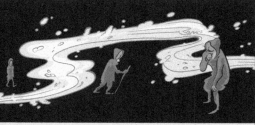

Say it like this: PATH-oh-jenz

The kinds of germs that get us **sick** can be spread from one person to another by a couple of methods. When you sneeze or cough, the particles of saliva or mucus* that spray out can carry germs with them. Germs can also live in blood and sweat, and can survive on surfaces that you encounter every day, like doorknobs, phones, handles.

Say it like this: MYOU-kuss

There are four types of germs:

*Bacteria** are tiny single-celled creatures. They can live inside or outside the body, and can cause ear infections, sore throats, and cavities. Not all are bad! Some "friendly" bacteria live in our intestines to help us digest food and make the most of a nutritious meal.

Scientists also use bacteria to make vaccines and medicines to *prevent* us from getting sick!

Say it like this: BAK-teer-ee-uh

VAK-seens

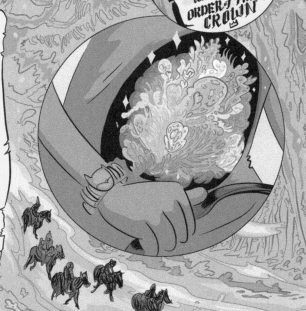

COUGH! COUGH!

Proclamation
GERMS: THE BAND of FOUR
Wanted by ORDER of THE CROWN

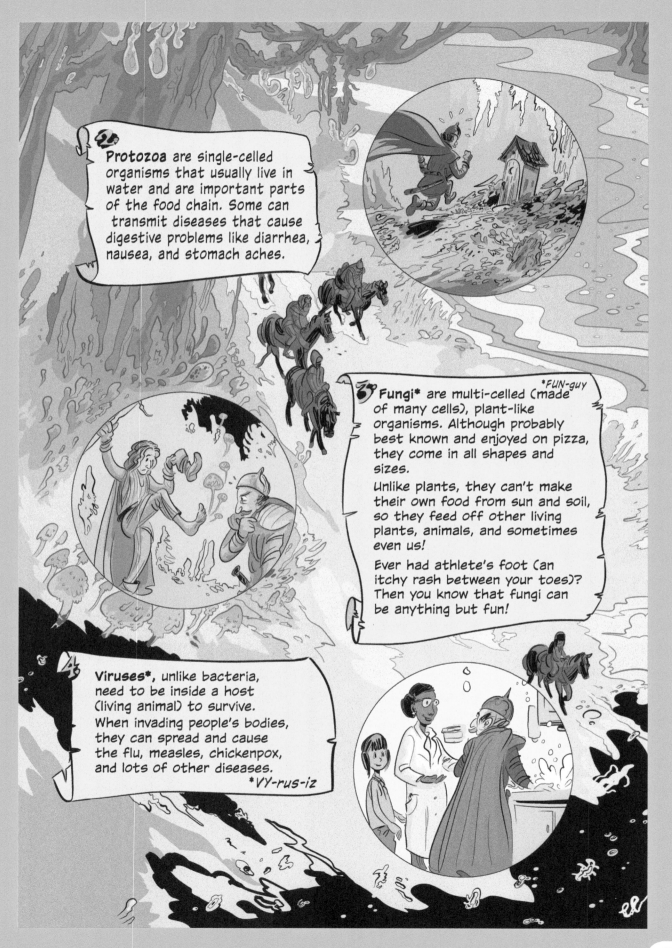

Protozoa are single-celled organisms that usually live in water and are important parts of the food chain. Some can transmit diseases that cause digestive problems like diarrhea, nausea, and stomach aches.

*FUN-guy

Fungi* are multi-celled (made of many cells), plant-like organisms. Although probably best known and enjoyed on pizza, they come in all shapes and sizes.

Unlike plants, they can't make their own food from sun and soil, so they feed off other living plants, animals, and sometimes even us!

Ever had athlete's foot (an itchy rash between your toes)? Then you know that fungi can be anything but fun!

Viruses*, unlike bacteria, need to be inside a host (living animal) to survive. When invading people's bodies, they can spread and cause the flu, measles, chickenpox, and lots of other diseases.

*VY-rus-iz

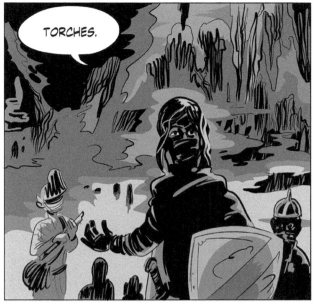

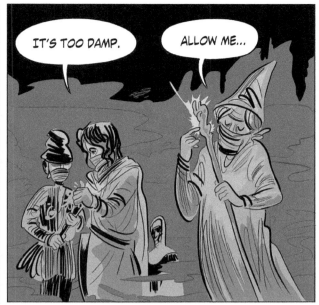

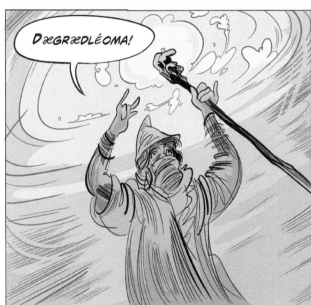

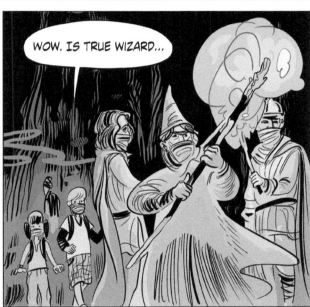

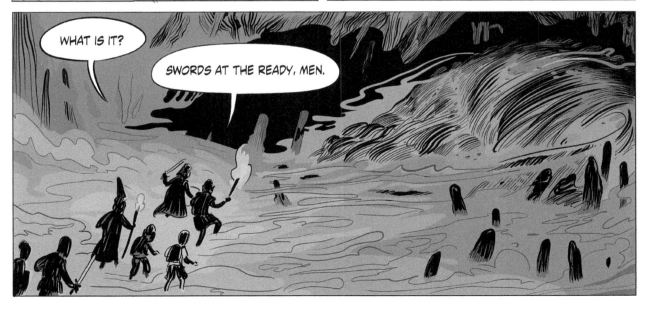

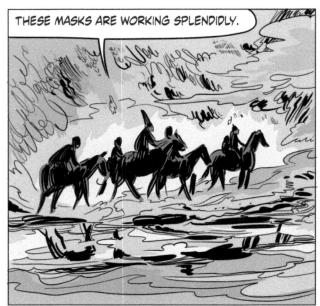

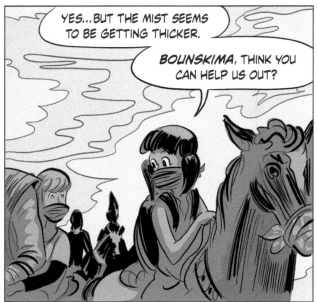

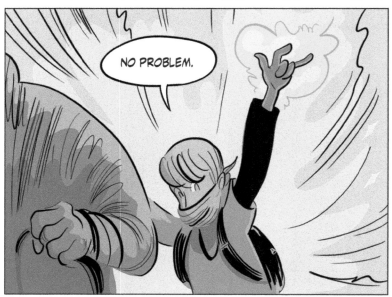

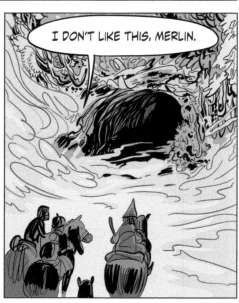

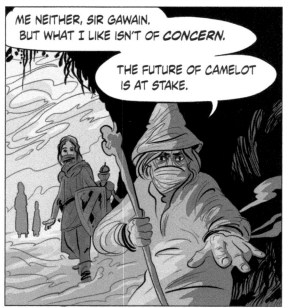

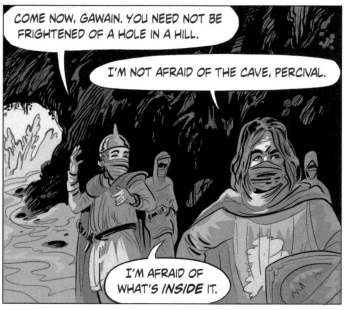

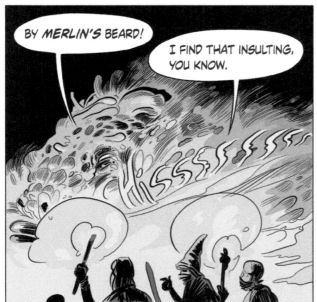

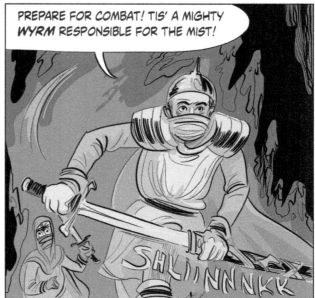

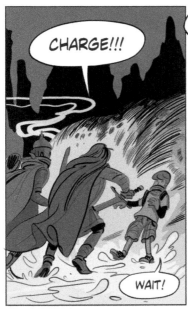

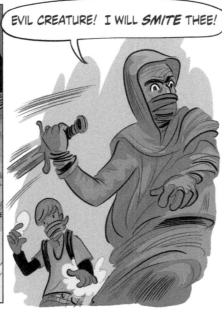

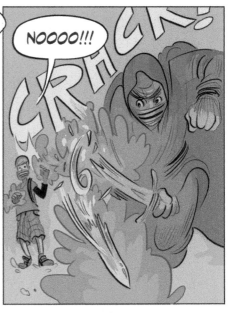

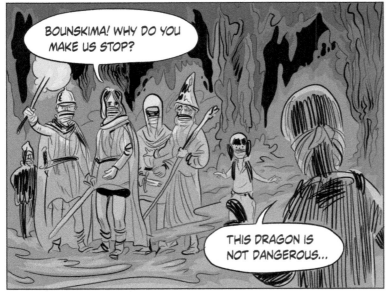

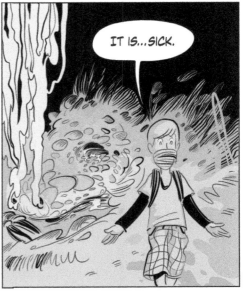

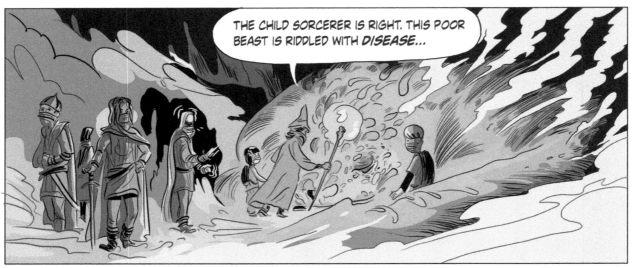

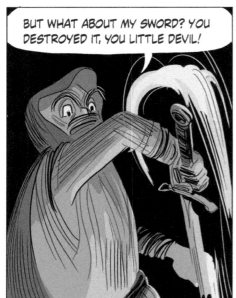

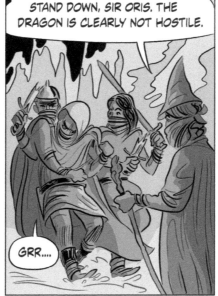

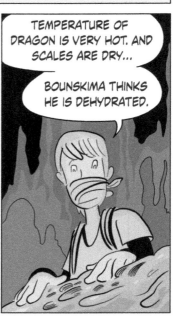

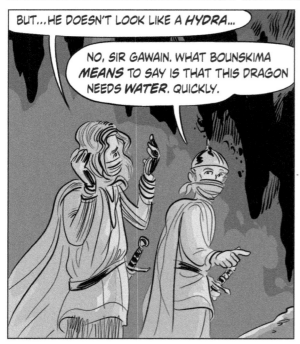

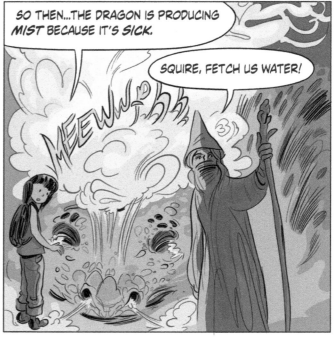

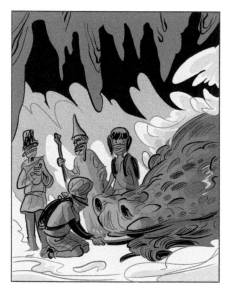

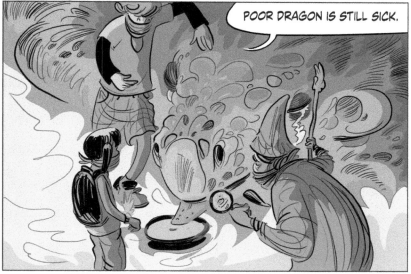

POOR DRAGON IS STILL SICK.

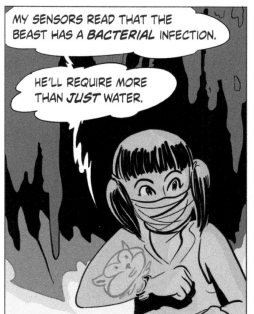

MY SENSORS READ THAT THE BEAST HAS A *BACTERIAL* INFECTION.

HE'LL REQUIRE MORE THAN *JUST* WATER.

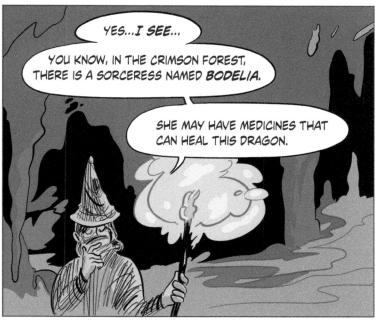

YES...*I SEE*...

YOU KNOW, IN THE CRIMSON FOREST, THERE IS A SORCERESS NAMED *BODELIA*.

SHE MAY HAVE MEDICINES THAT CAN HEAL THIS DRAGON.

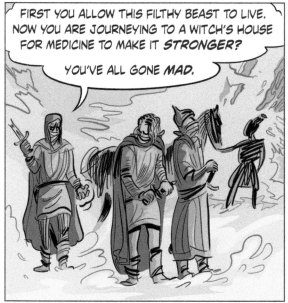

FIRST YOU ALLOW THIS FILTHY BEAST TO LIVE. NOW YOU ARE JOURNEYING TO A WITCH'S HOUSE FOR MEDICINE TO MAKE IT *STRONGER*?

YOU'VE ALL GONE *MAD*.

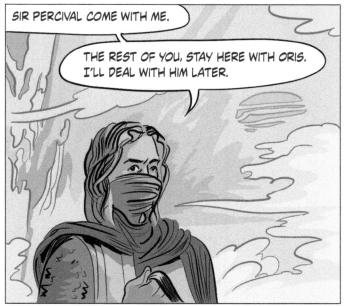

SIR PERCIVAL COME WITH ME.

THE REST OF YOU, STAY HERE WITH ORIS. I'LL DEAL WITH HIM LATER.

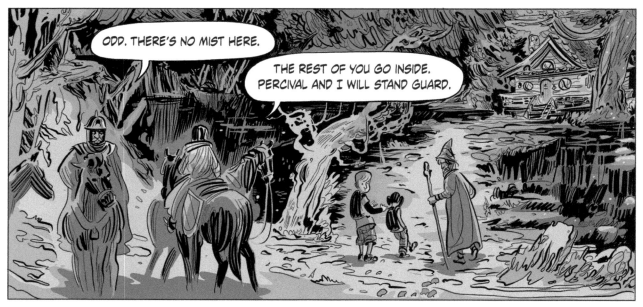

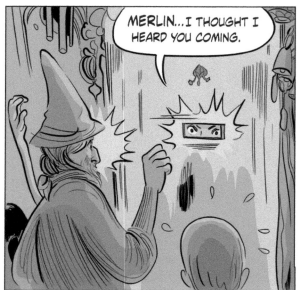

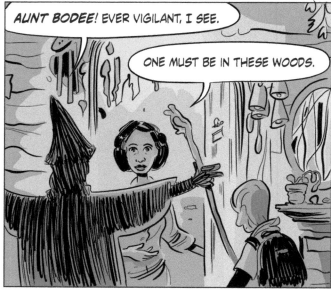

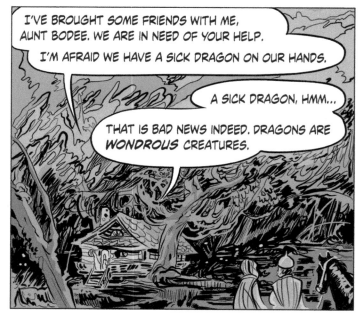

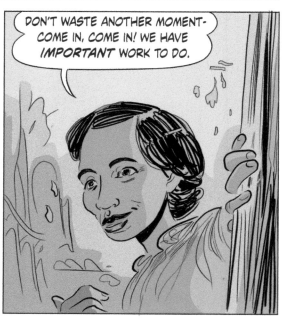

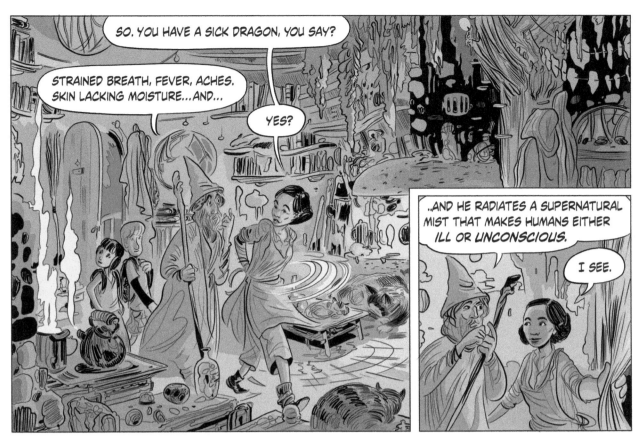

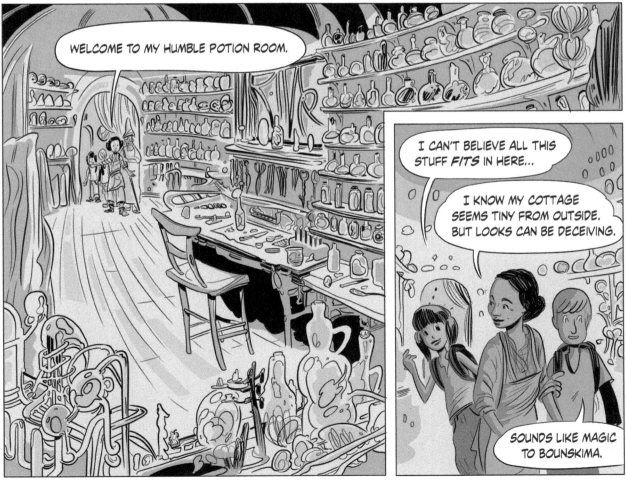

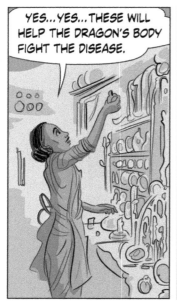

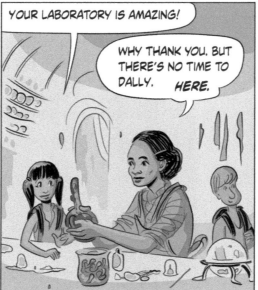

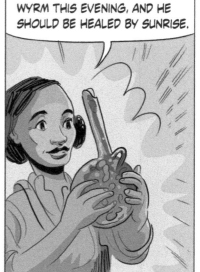

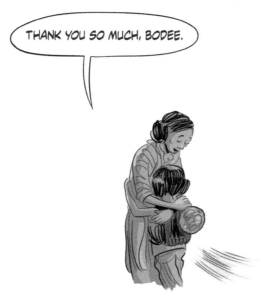

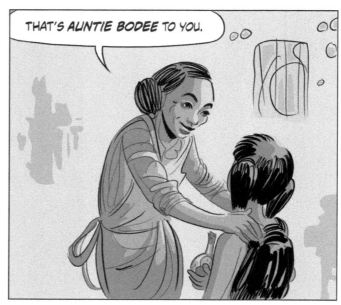

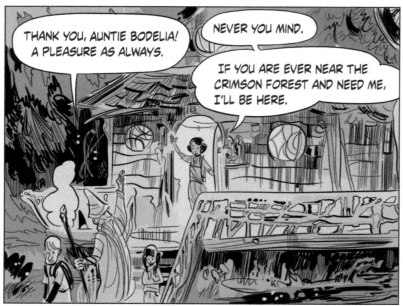

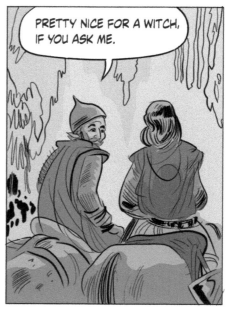

THE IMMUNE SYSTEM

With all these germs, your body needs lots of help keeping you healthy. Your "immune platoon" consists of the innate system and the adaptive system, both with many levels of protection. "Innate" means natural, something you are born with. Your **Innate System** is always there and always ready!

Believe it or not, your first line of defense is your skin. Its outer layer, the **epidermis**,* has 1) a living layer, the **dermis**, and 2) the topmost **stratum corneum** (Latin for "horny layer").

Built from dead cells like bricks and mortar, this layer effectively barricades against molecules and organisms we don't want to enter through our skin into our bloodstream.

Sometimes, germs sneak in through broken skin (cuts or scrapes), or your body needs to let things in, like when you eat, drink, smell, or digest. That's when your second line of defenses comes in.

*Say it like this: ep-id-DER-miss

Remember your tears and saliva from Adventure 5? Both have special chemicals called **enzymes**, which break down the cell walls of many bacteria and viruses that attempt to attack you.

Membranes in the mouth, throat, lungs, and intestines make a slimy substance, **mucus** (sometimes called "snot"). Did bacteria and viruses storm the gates? Mucus traps them! Your nose "runs" when you have a cold or flu partly because your body makes more mucus and fluid to wash away germs.

In your gut, stomach acid (also from Adventure 5!) not only aids the digestion process, but also helps kill harmful germs.

Even with all this, some germs can slip past your defenses, and eventually get you sick. That doesn't mean the war is over. In fact, this is when your immune system shows what it's really made of.

Lymph*, a clear fluid that carries white blood cells through the body, also collects bacteria or viruses. Lymph takes these germs to organs called "lymph nodes," where they are filtered and destroyed. You can often tell if you have an infection by checking the lymph nodes in your neck and under your arms. They swell up and get sensitive when you're sick, so you can feel them with your fingers, and they will probably hurt a little.

*Say it like this: limf

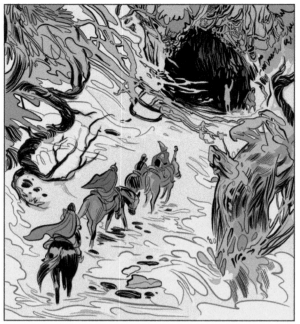
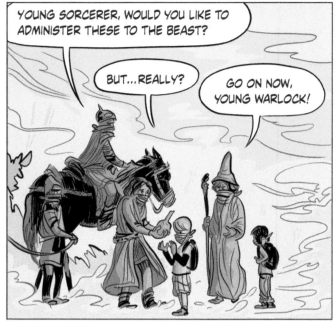
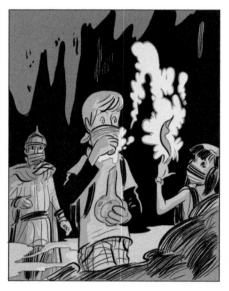
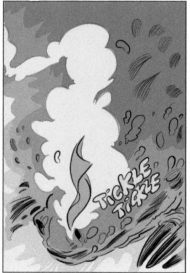
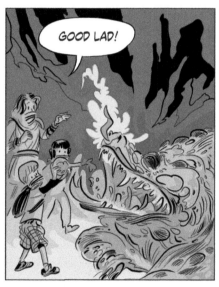
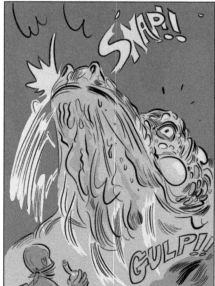
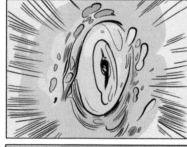
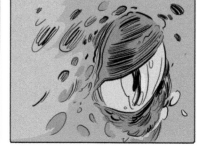
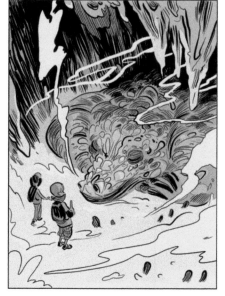

THE IMMUNE SYSTEM

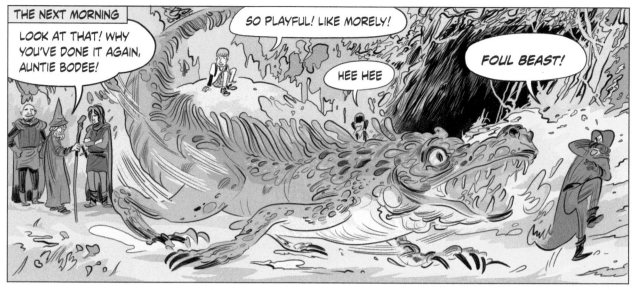

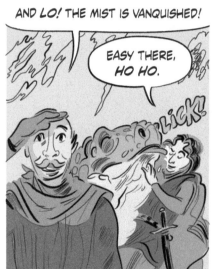

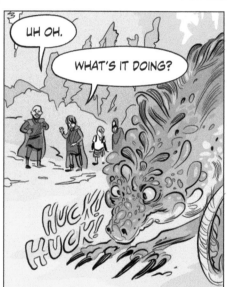

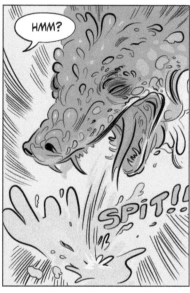

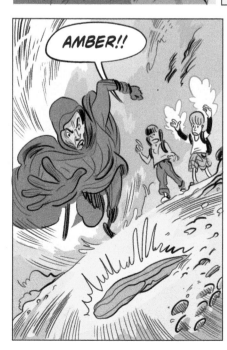

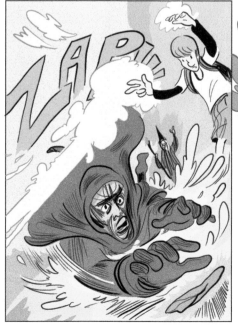

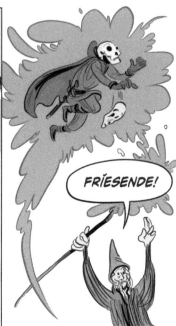

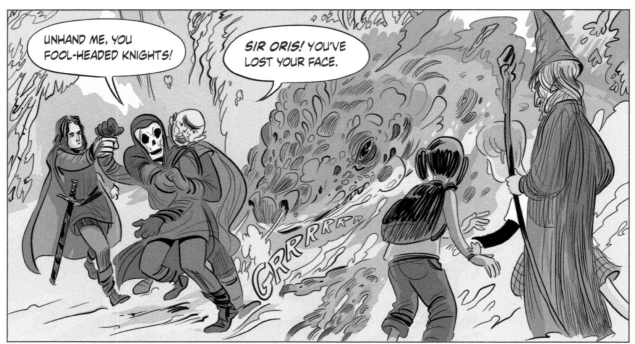

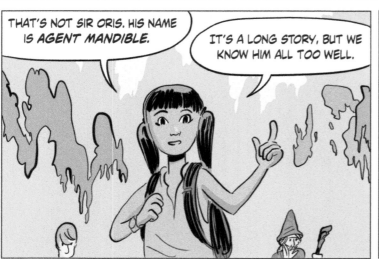

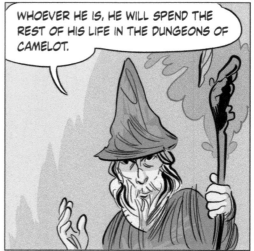

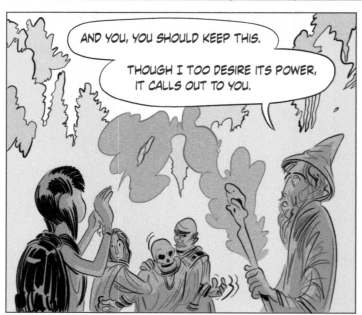

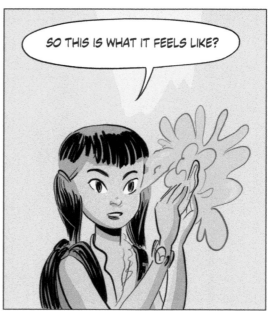

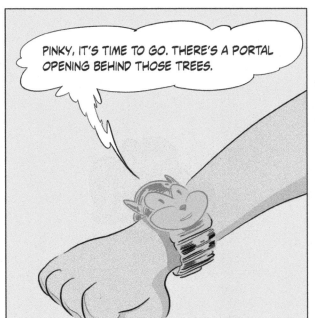

PINKY, IT'S TIME TO GO. THERE'S A PORTAL OPENING BEHIND THOSE TREES.

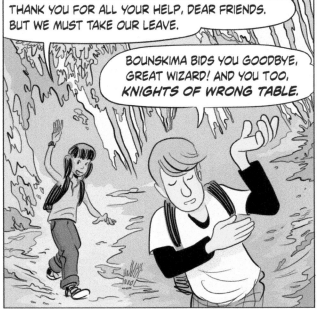

THANK YOU FOR ALL YOUR HELP, DEAR FRIENDS. BUT WE MUST TAKE OUR LEAVE.

BOUNSKIMA BIDS YOU GOODBYE, GREAT WIZARD! AND YOU TOO, **KNIGHTS OF WRONG TABLE.**

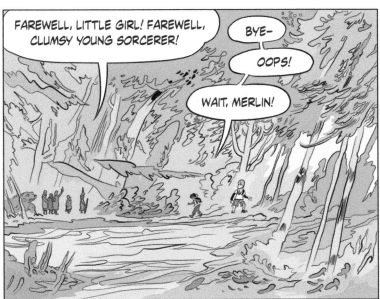

FAREWELL, LITTLE GIRL! FAREWELL, CLUMSY YOUNG SORCERER!

BYE— OOPS!

WAIT, MERLIN!

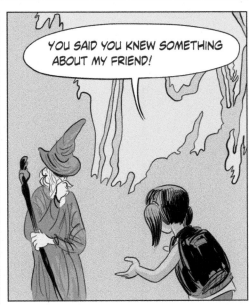

YOU SAID YOU KNEW SOMETHING ABOUT MY FRIEND!

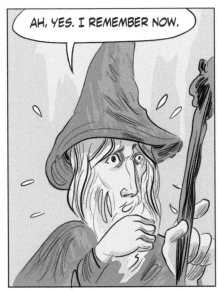

AH, YES. I REMEMBER NOW.

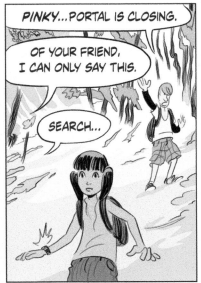

PINKY...PORTAL IS CLOSING.

OF YOUR FRIEND, I CAN ONLY SAY THIS.

SEARCH...

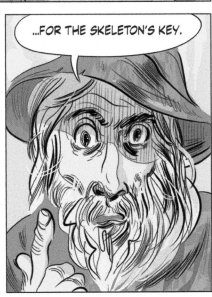

...FOR THE SKELETON'S KEY.

ADVENTURE 6

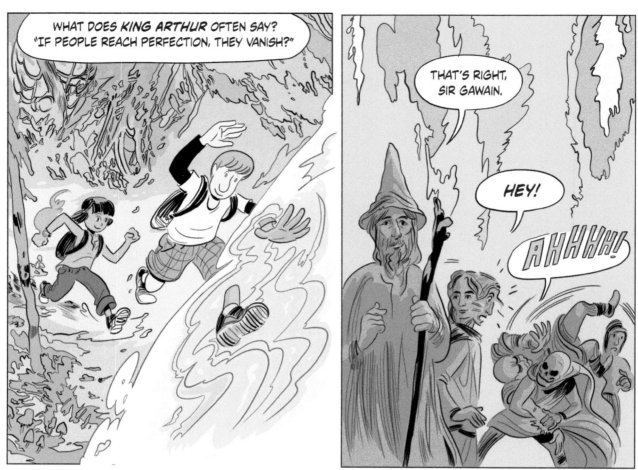

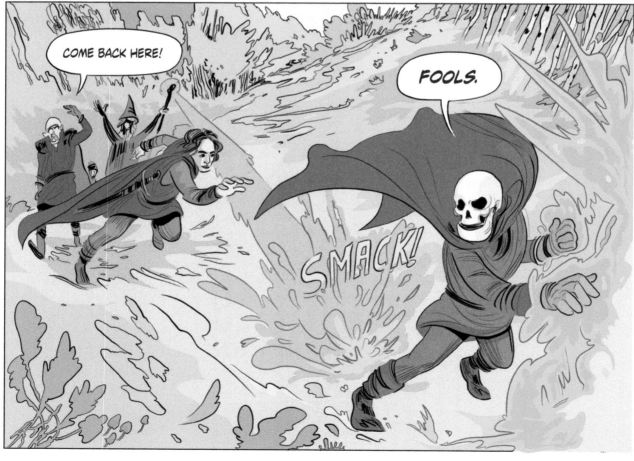

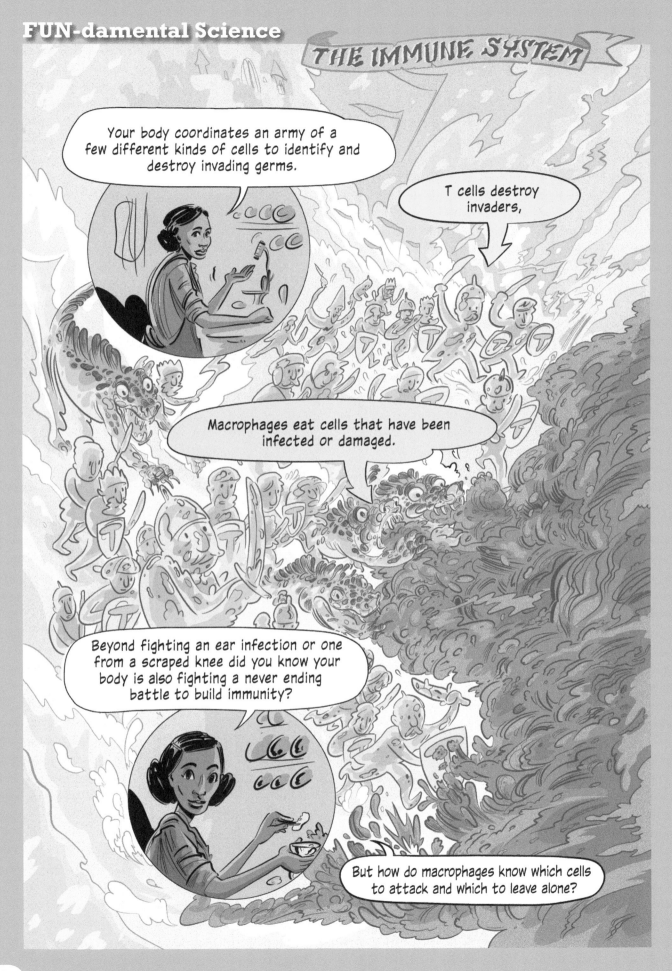

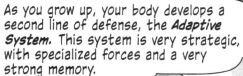
As you grow up, your body develops a second line of defense, the *Adaptive System*. This system is very strategic, with specialized forces and a very strong memory.

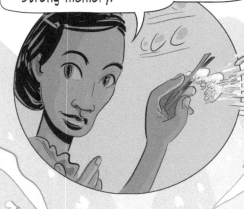

Special proteins called antibodies lock onto specific invaders. These antibodies stay in your body in case the germs return to the scene of the crime.

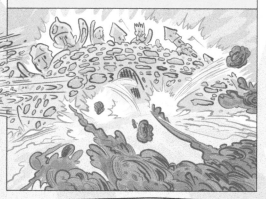

That's why most people only get sick from certain diseases like chickenpox once in their lives.

Immunizations can also help keep you healthy.

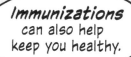

An immunization introduces weaker versions of antigens so your body recognizes them and generates antibodies without actually getting sick.

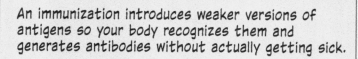

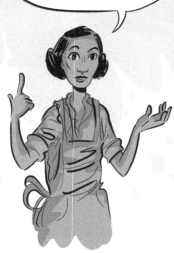

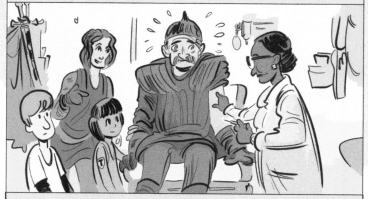

Once the antibodies are created, your T-cells are ready when it's really time to fight.

THE IMMUNE SYSTEM

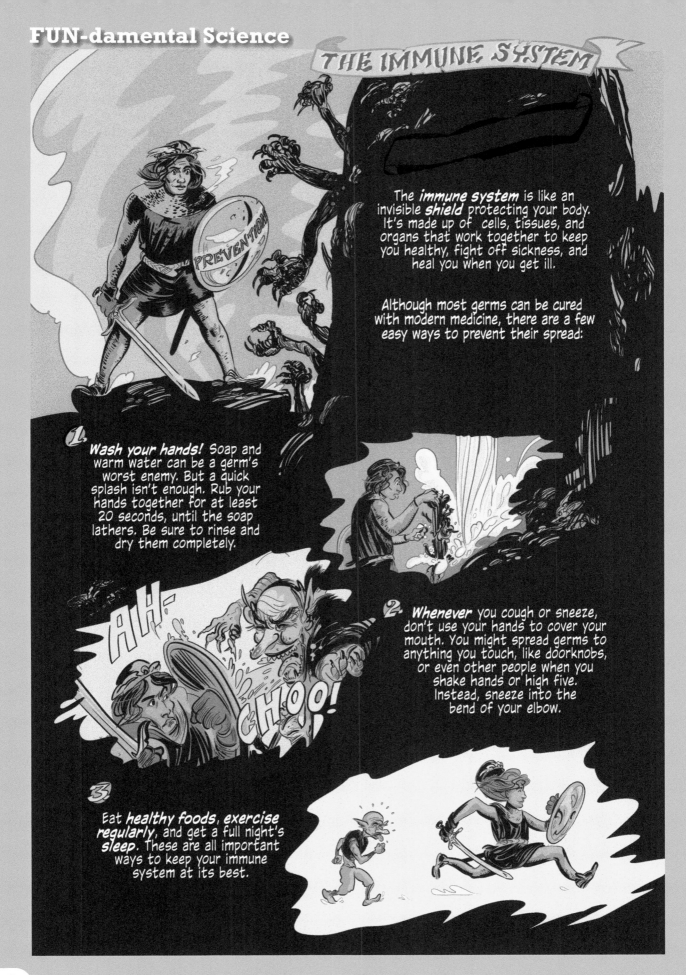

The *immune system* is like an invisible *shield* protecting your body. It's made up of cells, tissues, and organs that work together to keep you healthy, fight off sickness, and heal you when you get ill.

Although most germs can be cured with modern medicine, there are a few easy ways to prevent their spread:

1. *Wash your hands!* Soap and warm water can be a germ's worst enemy. But a quick splash isn't enough. Rub your hands together for at least 20 seconds, until the soap lathers. Be sure to rinse and dry them completely.

AH- CHOO!

2. *Whenever* you cough or sneeze, don't use your hands to cover your mouth. You might spread germs to anything you touch, like doorknobs, or even other people when you shake hands or high five. Instead, sneeze into the bend of your elbow.

3. Eat *healthy foods, exercise regularly*, and get a full night's *sleep*. These are all important ways to keep your immune system at its best.

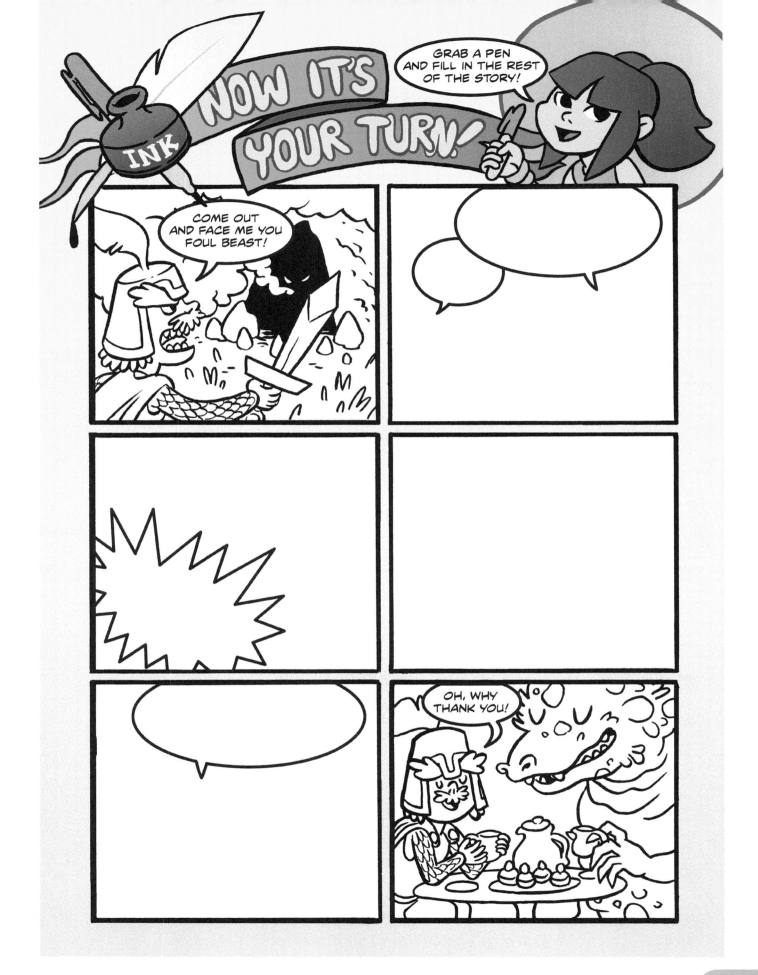

QUICK-START GUIDE
Learning Calendar

Part **1**

Know Your History

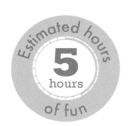
Estimated hours
5 hours of fun

Gather the adventure equipment you'll need from around the house - find the checklist on pages 46 and 47!

Locate England on a world map using a globe, an atlas, or an online map (e.g., https://geology.com/world/world-map.shtml) or check out Google Earth.

Read the comic **The Blights of Camelot** - find it at the beginning of this Adventure Guide!

Read *Know Your History*.

Read *Know Your Old English*.

Experience *Old English Calligraphy*.

Build *Your Own Fortress*.

Puzzle through *Arthurian England Crossword*.

Make *Your Myth*.

Part **2**

Know Your Immune System

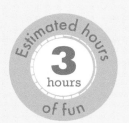
Estimated hours
3 hours of fun

Read *Know Your Immune System*.

Read *Bacteria Gone Wild* and complete *Strength in Numbers*.

Read *Know Your Hygiene* and complete *Clean Machine*.

Read *Hugs Not Bugs* and complete *Embraceable You*!

Read and complete *Fever Believer*.

Discover *Immune System Word Search*.

Dare to *Bolster your Defenses*.

Part 3
Know Your Appetite

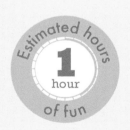

Read *Know Your Appetite*, shop for ingredients, and get your kitchen ready!

Prepare *Vegetable Pottage* and *Baked Apple with Oats*.

Share your dishes with your family. *Discuss Thoughts for Young Chefs* around the table!

Part 4
Show What You Know!

Knight School, Final Quest.

Congratulate Yourself *on a job well done!*

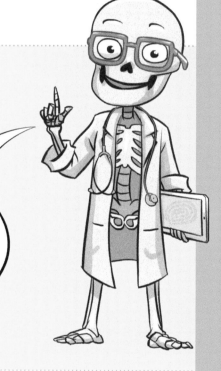

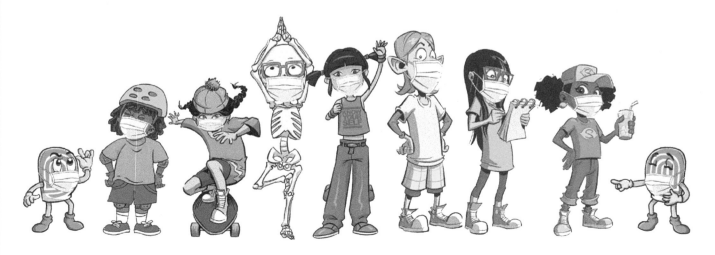

Home Inventory Checklist

Go on a scavenger hunt to find these items around the house.

These are the tools you will need on your adventure.

☐ **Paper**
- Old English Calligraphy

☐ **Colored pencils, markers, or crayons**
- Old English Calligraphy, DIY Coat of Arms, Build Your Own Fortress

☐ **Craft paint**
- Build Your Own Fortress

☐ **Empty boxes**
- Build Your Own Fortress

☐ **Cardboard cylinders (empty paper towel or toilet paper tubes)**
- Build Your Own Fortress

☐ **Toothpicks or wooden chopsticks**
- Build Your Own Fortress

☐ **Glue**
- Build Your Own Fortress

☐ **Scissors**
- Build Your Own Fortress

☐ **Wrapping paper, paper scraps, ribbon**
- Build Your Own Fortress

☐ **Tape**
- Build Your Own Fortress

☐ **Flour**
  - Handwashing - Clean Machine

☐ **Butter**
  - Handwashing - Clean Machine

☐ **Favorite Stuffed Animal**
  - Embraceable You

☐ **Thermometer**
  - Fever Believer

☐ **Two 10"x6" rectangles of cotton fabric**
  - DIY Face Masks

☐ **Two 6" pieces of elastic (or string, cloth strips, or hair ties)**
  - DIY Face Masks

☐ **Needle and thread (or bobby pin)**
  - DIY Face Masks

☐ **Scissors**
  - DIY Face Masks

☐ **Sewing Machine**
  - DIY Face Masks

☐ **Old T-Shirt**
  - No Sew T-Shirt

☐ **Old Bandana**
  - No Sew Bandana

☐ **Rubber Bands or Hair Ties**
  - No Sew Bandana

Be creative if you don't have something on the list.

✔ **Check them off when you have added them to your inventory!**

King Arthur

King Arthur is the perfect example of a character created from myth. A myth is a story, usually about the history of a people or a place, that might be based on some factual information but is also fictionalized to help establish a clear moral or message. Because of this, the line between truth and make believe in myths is often very blurry.

The earliest legends about Arthur from the fifth and sixth century suggest that he is based on a real person, but those who've studied the history of ancient England have yet to determine who that person might have been.

Regardless of whether he was real or not, countless stories have formed around him, including having magical powers learned from Merlin the Magician. The best known myth, about him as a courtly medieval king, didn't develop until almost half a millennium later, in the twelfth century!

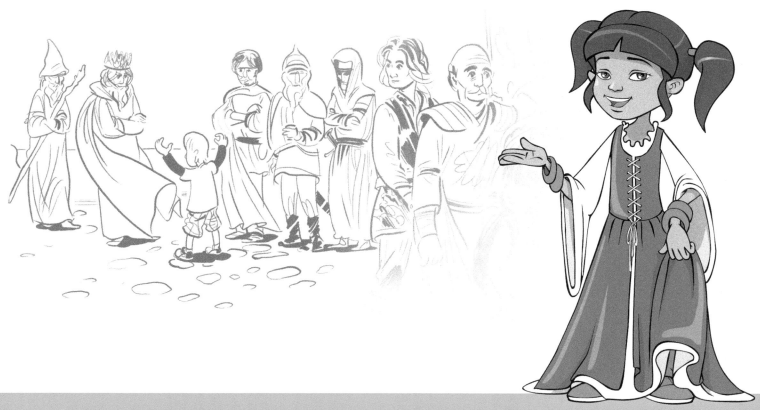

Knights of the Round Table

Knights of the Round Table were the most skilled warriors in the kingdom of Camelot, a mythical town of castles, forests, and meadows located in Great Britain. If you wanted to become a Knight of the Round Table, you had to prove you were chivalrous, meaning courteous and considerate. In fact, the knights had to swear to a Code of Chivalry, which is similar to the oath that doctors take to help and protect their patients (known as the Hippocratic Oath). This meant they had to promise to uphold and enforce the rules of Camelot, which was their responsibility to protect. They gathered at a special table that was round, rather than rectangular, so that everyone who sat around it would be seen as an equal.

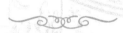

The Dark Ages

"The Dark Ages," as the name suggests, is part of England's history characterized by violence, starvation, and disaster.

No longer under the rule of the Roman Empire after 400 CE, England, and much of Europe, fell into chaos. Historical records are hazy for a lot of the Dark Ages, but war was common and England had to combat constant attacks from roaming bands of invaders. Kings and Lords lived in luxury compared to the majority of the people.

Hygiene and medicine were significantly less developed than they are now; plagues, famine, and other health issues were common. It is quite amazing that England, as a sovereign nation, evolved out of the Dark Ages, which lasted ten centuries!

Know Your Old English

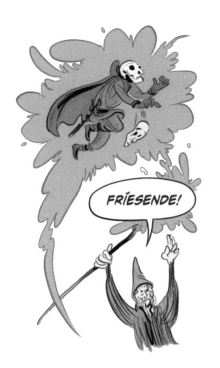

FRÍESENDE!

Did you notice the word "wyrm" in Time Skaters 6? That's Old English for dragon. Or, how about when Merlin said "friesende!" that means "freeze!"

Here are a few other fun words, Old English style:

Durst - to be daring or bold enough to enact something

Whither - to where

Imagine Pinky and Bounski practicing Old English...

Durst we approach the wyrm? Is it friend or foe?

Whither thou goest Pinky, I go.

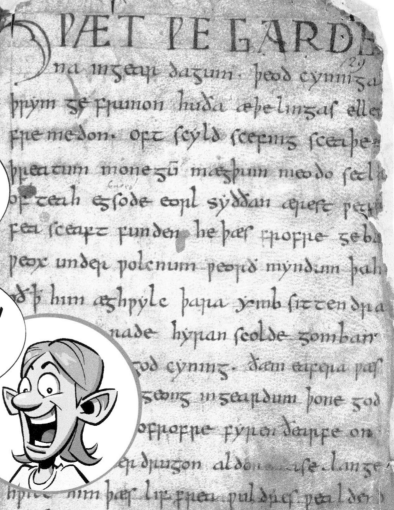

A page from the original Beowulf

If this Adventure Guide existed in the Middle Ages, only monks and the most highly educated people would be able to read it. We couldn't read it either, because the Anglo-Saxons used a language we call Old English. Old English, also called Anglo-Saxon, is the language spoken by the English inhabitants of Britain from about 500 to 1100 CE Much of Old English doesn't even look like English at all.

Beowulf is a very famous poem written in Old English. The opening line, shown below, means "over the whale's road." What kind of road could that be?

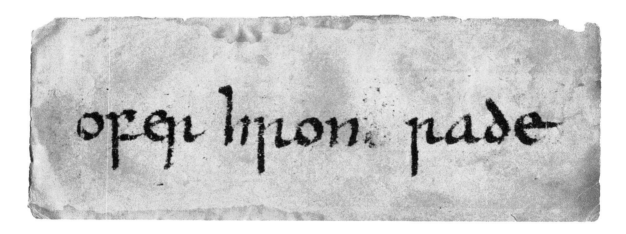

Not only was literacy a privilege, but since the printing press hadn't been invented yet, books had to be copied by hand! Only a few people knew how to write, and the process of copying a text took a long time. On the plus side, writing by hand allowed people to develop beautiful styles of text.

Now you can practice writing this Old English letter:

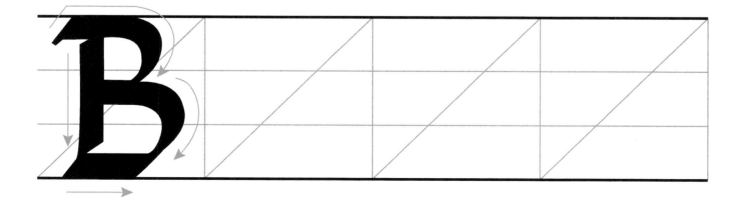

Old English Calligraphy

Materials:

- **Printed templates on the next pages**

- **Scrap paper**

- **Washable markers**
  (or a calligraphy pen if you have one!)

Directions:

- Use the calligraphy templates to trace letters in an Old English writing style.

- Practice writing the letters of your name on scrap paper.

- Create a nameplate for yourself using the dragon template.
  Get creative with colors and decorations!

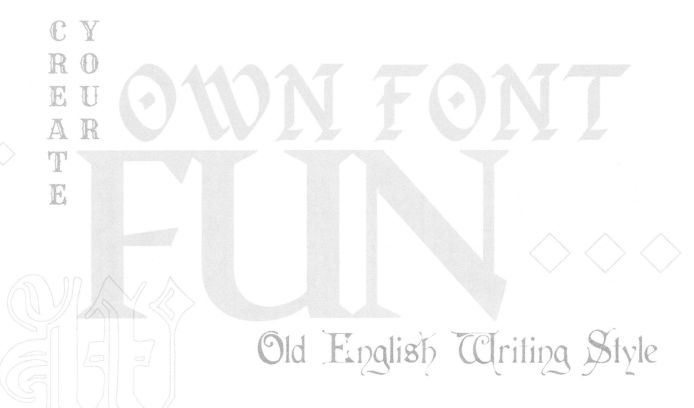

CREATE YOUR OWN FONT FUN

Old English Writing Style

Old English Calligraphy Template - Simple

A B C D

E F G H

I J K L M

N O P Q

R S T U V

W X Y Z

Old English Calligraphy Template - Advanced

Aa Bb Cc Dd

Ee Ff Gg Hh

Ii Jj Kk Ll Mm

Nn Oo Pp Qq

Rr Ss Tt Uu Vv

Ww Xx Yy Zz

Old English Calligraphy Practice Sheet

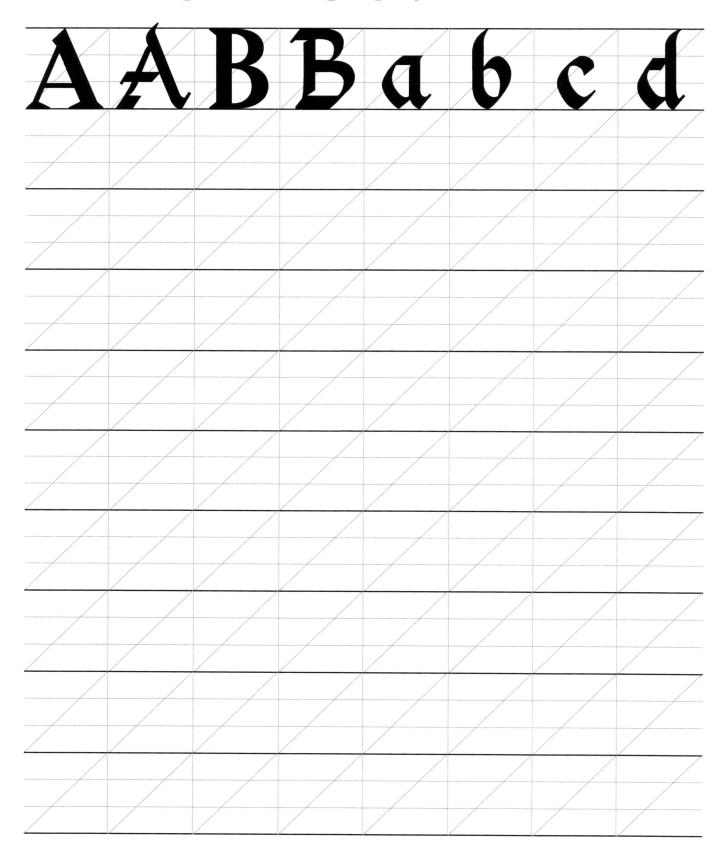

Old English Calligraphy Practice Sheet

Design Your Own Font

Now that you have had some practice,
design your own font here:

Name The Dragon

Now that you have had some practice, write this dragon's name on the line with a calligraphy style of your choosing.

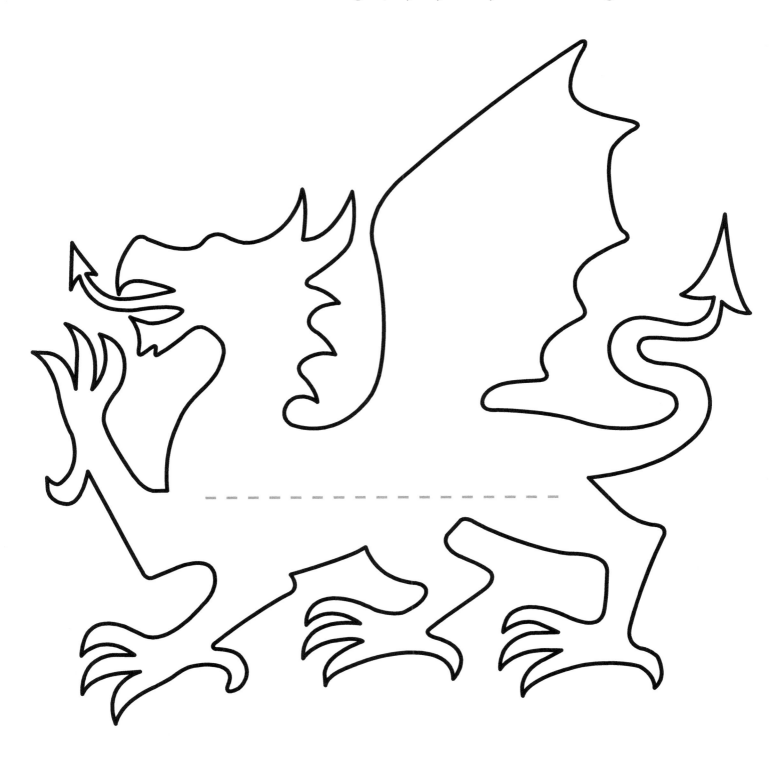

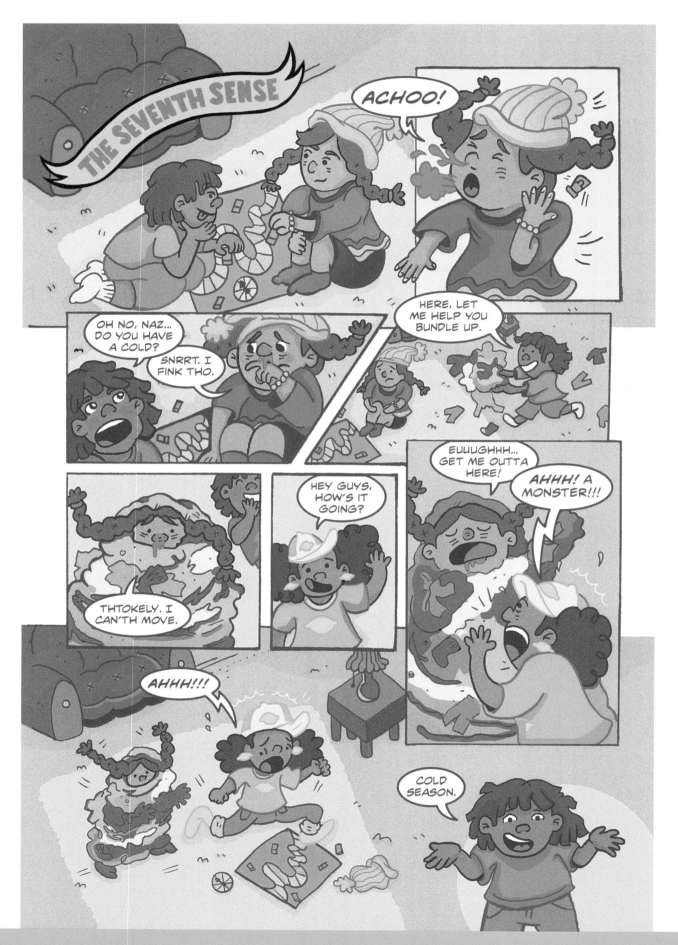

Know Your Coat of Arms

A coat of arms is a design that combines images and symbols that are important to a person, group, or country. These designs were commonly featured on shields, flags, and other highly visible materials.

Here are some common symbols from the Middle Ages to choose from, or you can look up "*coat of arms symbols and their meanings*" for more ideas.

Wolves – nature, freedom

Swords – courage, bravery, strength in battle

Holy grail – eternal life

Crown – power, wealth

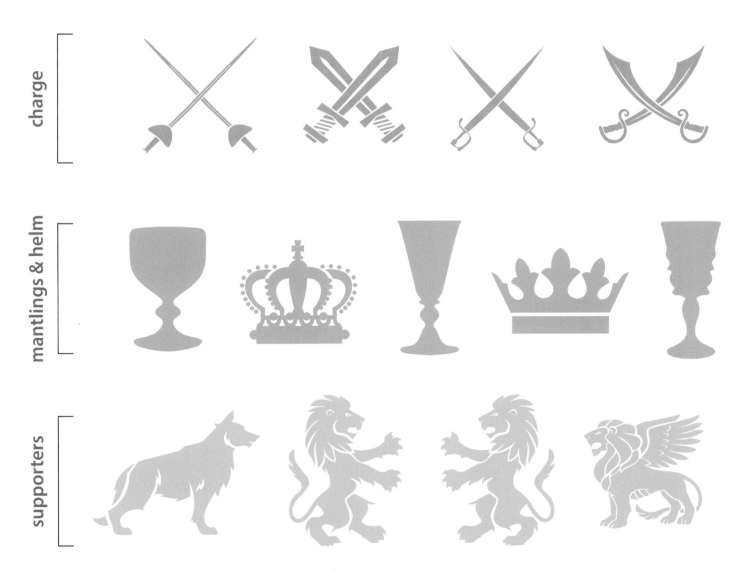

charge

mantlings & helm

supporters

DIY Coat of Arms

Materials:

- **Colored pencils or crayons**
- **The template on page 63**

Directions:

1. Choose a color for your crest. Traditional colors were red, blue, green, purple, and grey.

2. Choose a "charge" to sketch on the front of the crest, or trace one of the symbols provided. For example: A charge might be swords, because they represent a personal characteristic or trait.

3. Add some styling to the top of your crest with mantlings and helm. Often found on a knight's cloak, the mantlings were fancy decorations, and the helm acted as a knight's mark or what we might refer to today as your "avatar."

4. Lastly, who or what is in your "Round Table"? Choose your supporters and add them to the outsides of your crest, bottom left and bottom right. For exampke, they could be lions adding a solid foundation to your efforts in knighthood.

5. Add a phrase or motto to represent your character and strength.

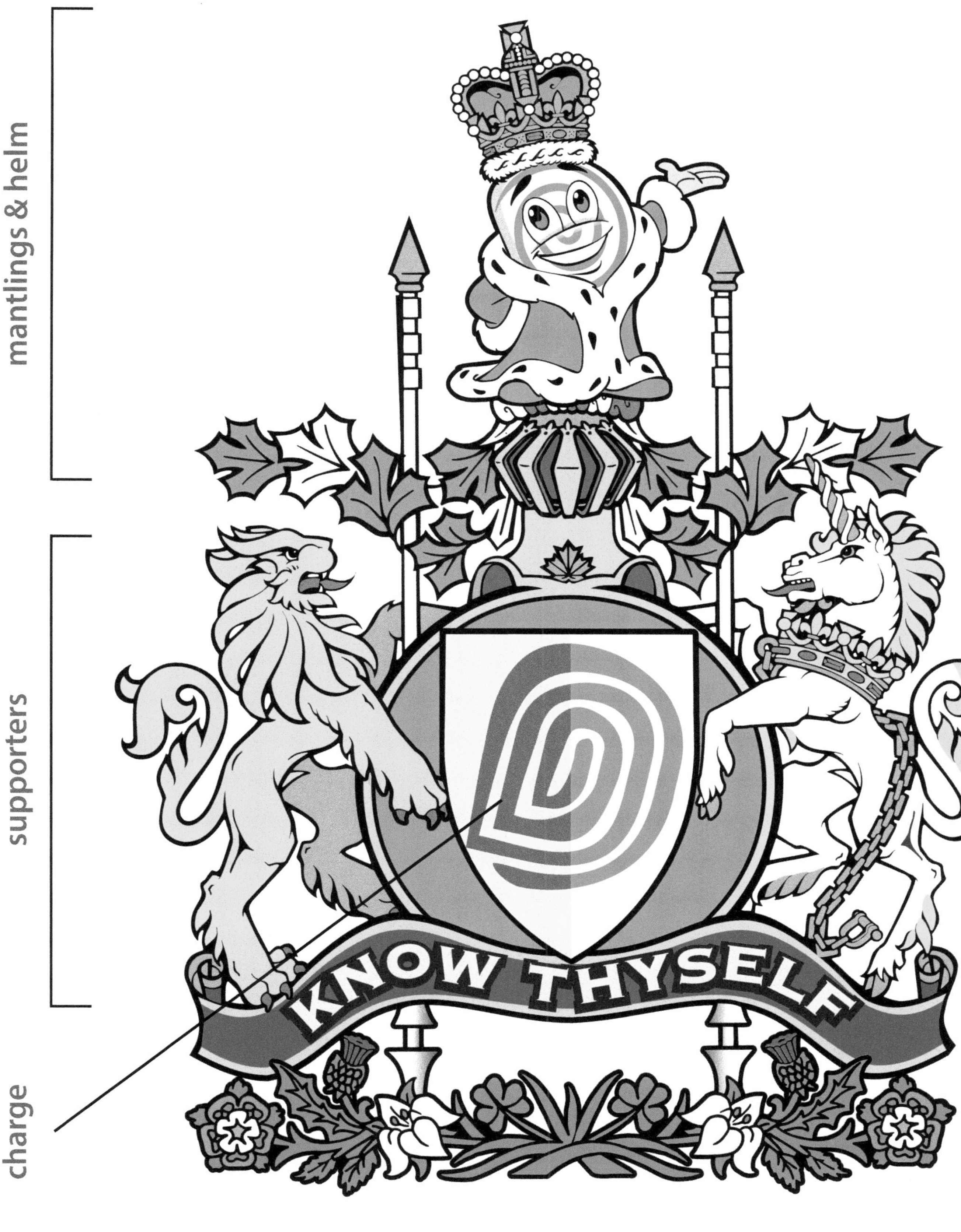

mantlings & helm

supporters

charge

KNOW THYSELF

Coat of Arms Template

Have fun building your original Coat of Arms below
using the previous three pages as a guide.

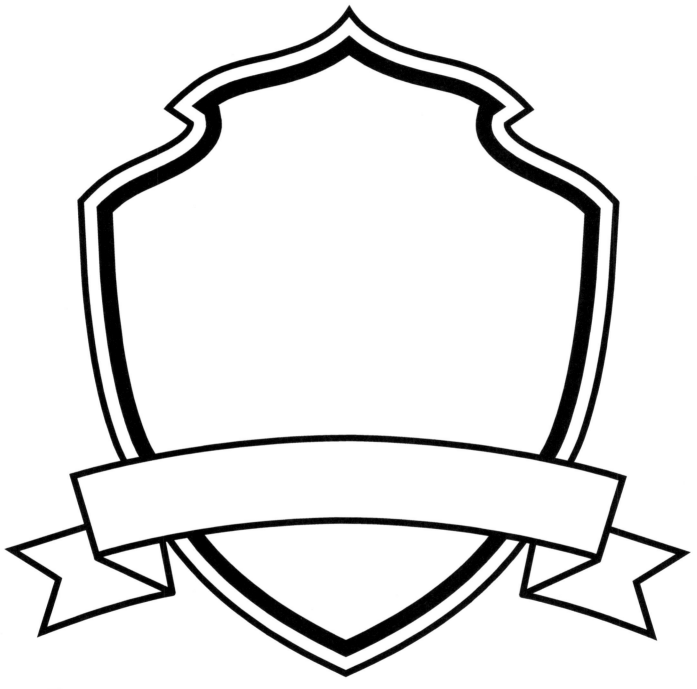

 Make sure to have a grown up take a photo and share your fortress
on social media using the hashtag #KnowYourAdventure!

KnowYourselfOAK   KnowYourselfOAK

Build Your Own Fortress

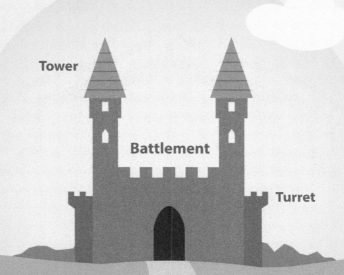

Tower

Battlement

Turret

Materials:

- **Paint**

- **Empty cardboard boxes**
  Assorted sizes, ask your parents for used boxes

- **Cardboard cylinders**
  Look for spare paper towel or toilet paper tubes

- **Wrapping paper, paper scraps, ribbons**
  These will be used to decorate your very own castle, so get creative!

- **Washable liquid glue, glue sticks, and/or hot glue gun**

- **Scissors**

- **Tape**

ADVENTURE 6

Directions:

- Choose your largest box and tape the bottom closed. Cut the top flaps off. Cut out battlements around the top perimeter and window arches on the front and sides. Repeat with additional boxes, if desired.

- Paint the boxes a solid color and let dry.

- Use markers, colored pencils, crayons, and/or paint to decorate the interior and exterior of your boxes.

- Use your cardboard boxes and cylinders to create doors, turrets, pillars, and more!

- Cut triangles out of scrap paper. Glue or tape them to toothpicks or wooden chopsticks to decorate your castle. Think about flags, battlements, windows, banners and glue flags to your castle battlements.

- Use ribbon and/or extra strips of paper to drape your castle's battlements and windows with banners and garlands.

- Optional - Glue your Coat of Arms to one of your castle walls for an extra personalized look. Populate your fortress by adding characters!

 Make sure to have your grown up take a photo and share on social media using the hashtag #KnowYourAdventure!

 KnowYourselfOAK   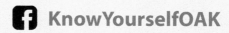 KnowYourselfOAK

Make Your Myth

Don't make any *myth*-takes!

Now that you have learned a bit about the Middle Ages and the mystical world of King Arthur, demonstrate what you know by making up a story about yourself as a knight or lady knight in a medieval myth.

What would your name and title be?

_____

_____

_____

What kingdom would you live in, and what would it look like?

_____

_____

_____

_____

_____

_____

_____

_____

_____

What types of quests would you go on? What character traits would you be known for?

_____

_____

_____

_____

_____

_____

_____

_____

Discuss the meaning of the symbols you included on your coat of arms.

_____

_____

_____

_____

_____

_____

_____

_____

Arthurian England Crossword

This crossword puzzle is a chance for you to show what you have learned.

Give it a shot!

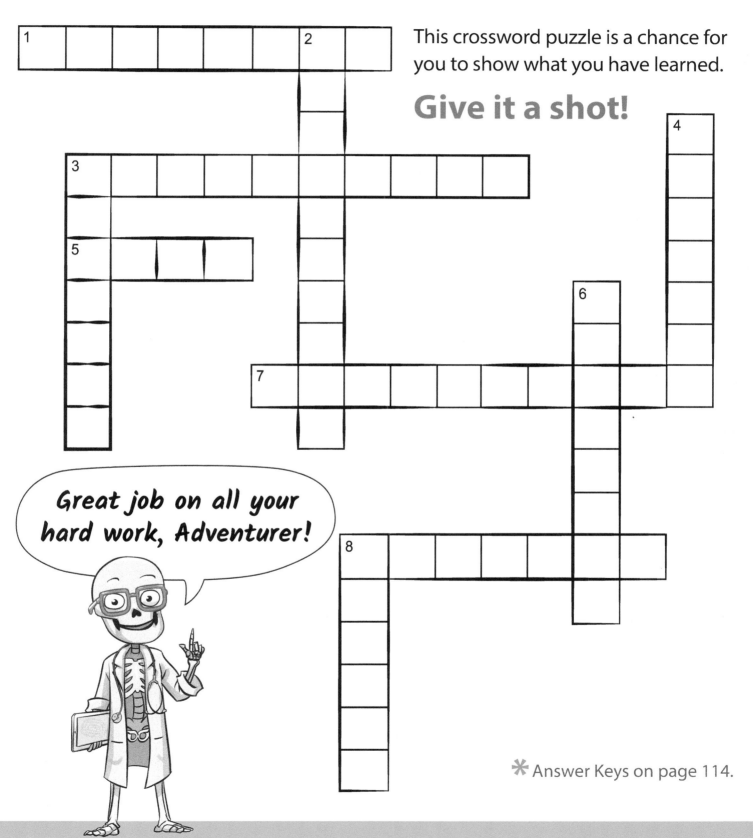

Great job on all your hard work, Adventurer!

* Answer Keys on page 114.

Across:

1. The historical period in which the myths of King Arthur were set.

3. Meaning 'courteous and considerate'.

5. A story, maybe based on some factual information, meant to deliver a moral or message.

7. A crest displaying symbolism important to a person, group, or country.

8. Old English for 'to where'.

Down:

2. Language spoken by English inhabitants of Britain in the Middle Ages.

3. Mythical kingdom of Arthurian England.

4. _____ of the Round Table.

6. A historical period of England's history characterized by violence, starvation, and disaster.

8. Symbolized nature and freedom on crests in the Middle Ages.

Know Your Immune System

Like an invisible shield, the immune system protects you from germs and illness. It's made of cells, tissues, and organs that work together to keep you healthy. You might think of things like swelling or fever as signs of infection, but they are actually signs your immune system is working. When bacteria or viruses penetrate your skin through a cut or opening and start multiplying inside your body, different types of white blood cells rally to your body's defense.

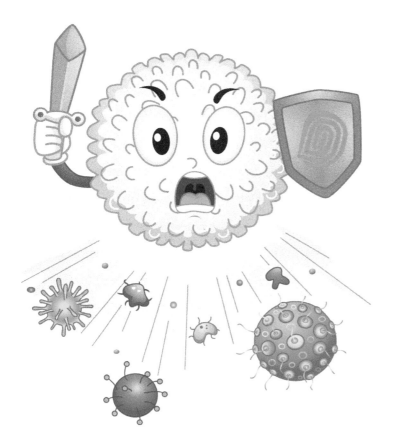

When your immune system finds germs or any substances that aren't part of your body, white blood cells coordinate to attack the invaders and also remember how to react to a specific invader in the future.

White blood cells, also known as **leukocytes***, start out in your bone marrow, growing from stem cells, and can also be found in your blood and lymph. There are different kinds of leukocytes, each with a different job in the immune army.

White Blood Cells
(Leukocytes)

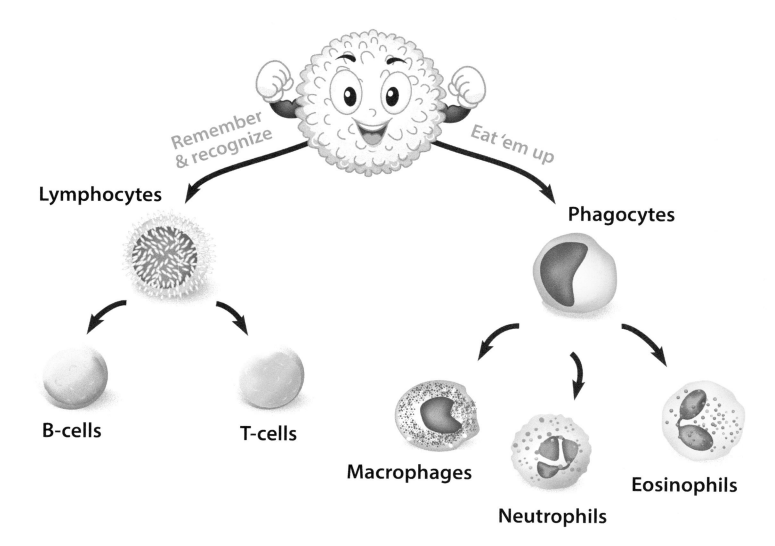

There are two types of leukocytes: lymphocytes and phagocytes. Lymphocytes "remember and recognize" while phagocytes "eat up" invaders.

There are different types of phagocytes like **macrophages*** and **neutrophils***. The neutrophils move around your blood, look for antigens, and create a liquid known as pus to help eat up bacteria in a wound. They're the biggest group of all the white blood cells.

Macrophages*, the largest in size of white blood cells, live in different parts of your body. They are responsible for detecting, devouring, and destroying pathogens. Other phagocytes, like eosinophils, direct cell movements, like a general directing troops.

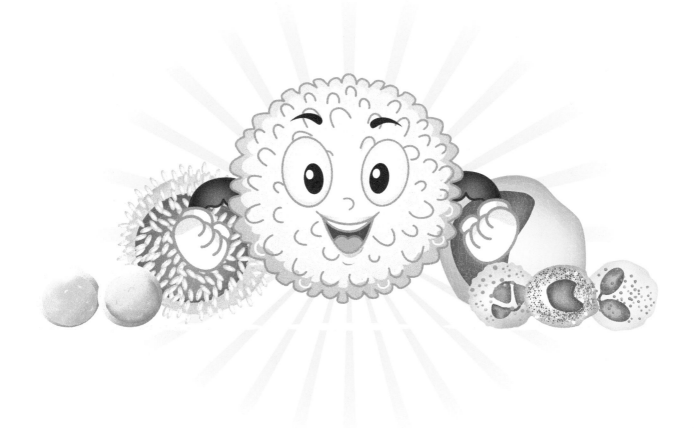

While the battle is raging, the cells on the frontlines send a "call to arms" for other cells such as lymphocytes. There are two types: **T cells**, which help attack invaders, and **B cells**, makers of antibodies, which identify and neutralize bacteria and viruses.

Cells are labeled with a "human leukocyte antigen" (HLA); working like a uniform, it helps the immune system identify and protect. When your immune system recognizes the HLA "uniform," it does not attack. Without this uniform your immune system gathers the troops.

When not on alert or battling invaders, your immune system is naturally keeping you healthy.

A mass of good bacteria (100 trillion, in fact!) lives in your large colon as a system of its own called the **microbiome**, and is unique to each person. Even though your body is on the lookout for bad bacteria, nurturing the good bacteria in your gut also supports and strengthens your immunity.

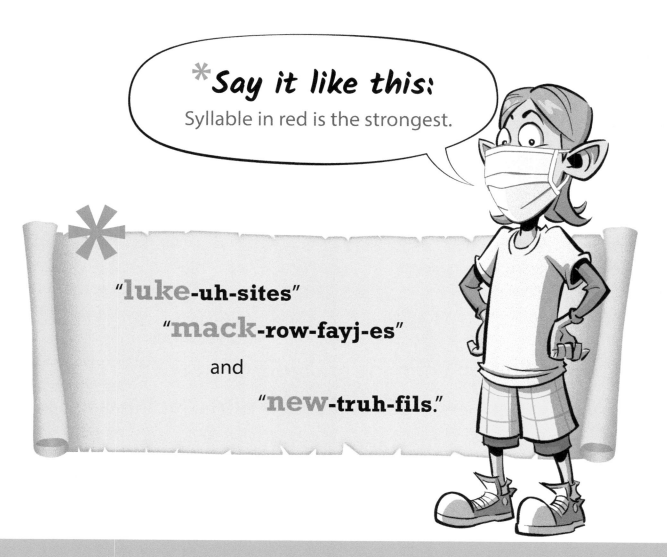

*Say it like this:
Syllable in red is the strongest.

"luke-uh-sites"

"mack-row-fayj-es"

and

"new-truh-fils."

Bacteria Gone Wild

Which is bigger?

Two germs growing exponentially like this, 2^5, or multiplying like this, 2×5?

One of the reasons germs and bacteria, in particular, can be so alarming is because they multiply like crazy! Unlike regular multiplication by just one number, this kind of growth is way more powerful.

We can represent the results using exponents, often called "powers," and, in this case, the base number 2. Your lymphocytes and phagocytes know all about bacteria's so-called "powers." They work together to fight invading germs before exponential growth really takes over, your temperature rises, and you have to call in a supporting cast of doctors and medicine.

Here's an example of bacteria gone wild! Once it's reached a total number of 128, simple remedies may no longer work. Can you fill in the blanks and determine which day that is?

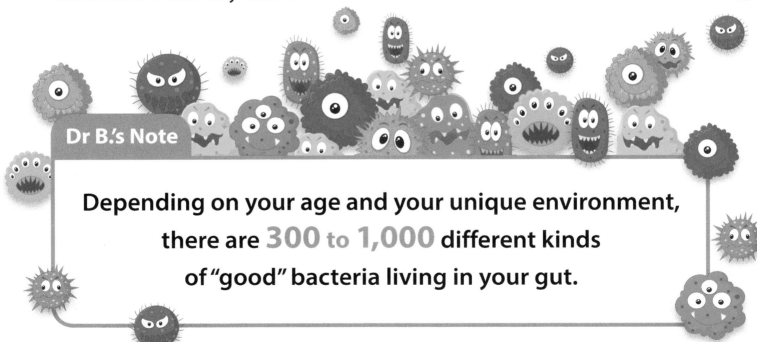

Dr B.'s Note

Depending on your age and your unique environment, there are 300 to 1,000 different kinds of "good" bacteria living in your gut.

Strength in Numbers

Show off what you have learned. Fill in the blanks below.

What day is it?	How are the bacteria growing?	How many copies of 2 get multiplied by itself?	What is the total number of bacteria?	How is growth written with exponents?
0	1	0	1	2^0
1	2	1	2	2^1
2	2x2			2^2
3	2x2x2		8	
4			16	2^4
5	2x2x2x2x2	5		
6				2^6
7		7		
8				

Know Your Hygiene

Hygiene is the term for all the things you do to keep yourself clean and healthy. It includes everything from washing your hands with soap and water to cleaning your room and taking out the trash.

Since most viruses can't stay alive for a long time outside of a host (your body, in this activity), washing your hands before you rub your eyes or eat food will help to ensure you don't accidentally spread any germs.

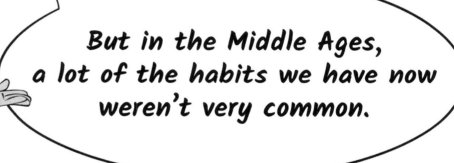

But in the Middle Ages, a lot of the habits we have now weren't very common.

During this time, crusaders brought soap back from Turkey and other parts of Western Asia.

Even with soap, the average Western European only bathed about once a month or less, mainly because clean water wasn't readily available and because many people held superstitions about water being harmful to them.

World Health Organization's Proper Hand-Washing Guidelines

The best way to protect yourself from infection and to avoid spreading germs to others is to wash your hands correctly and frequently. Find the World Health Organization's (WHO) guidelines for proper hand-washing below.

1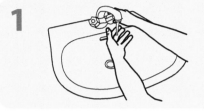

Wet hands with water

2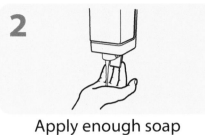

Apply enough soap
to cover all

3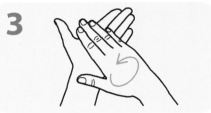

Rub hands palm to palm

4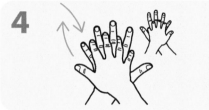

Right palm over left dorsum
with interlaced fingers
and vice versa

5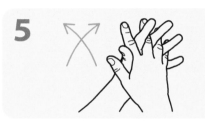

Palm to palm
with fingers interlaced

6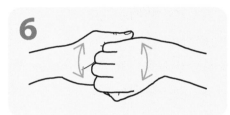

Backs of fingers
to opposing palms
with fingers interlocked

7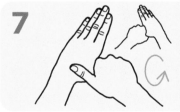

Rotational rubbing
of left thumb clasped in
right palm and vice versa

8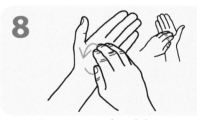

Rotational rubbing,
backwards and forwards
with clasped fingers of right

9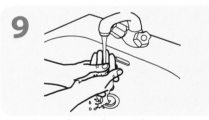

Rinse hands with water

10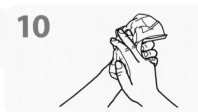

Dry hands thoroughly
with a single use towel

11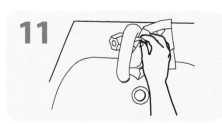

Use towel to turn off faucet

12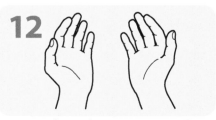

Your hands are now safe

Clean Machine

Materials:

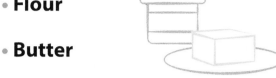

- **Flour**
- **Butter**

Directions:

1. Coat your hands first in butter followed by flour.

2. Turn on the faucet and rinse your hands (use your wrists so you don't get anything on the handles).

3. Once your hands are wet, turn the faucet off and get a little soap.

4. Begin to recite the Dr. Bonyfide Hand Rap (or start counting loud) while you scrub your hands until you work up a lather and see bubbles and suds.

5. Repeat the rap while you make sure you get between your fingers and under fingernails.

6. Keep scrubbing and sudsing until all the butter and flour is gone and your hands are smooth.

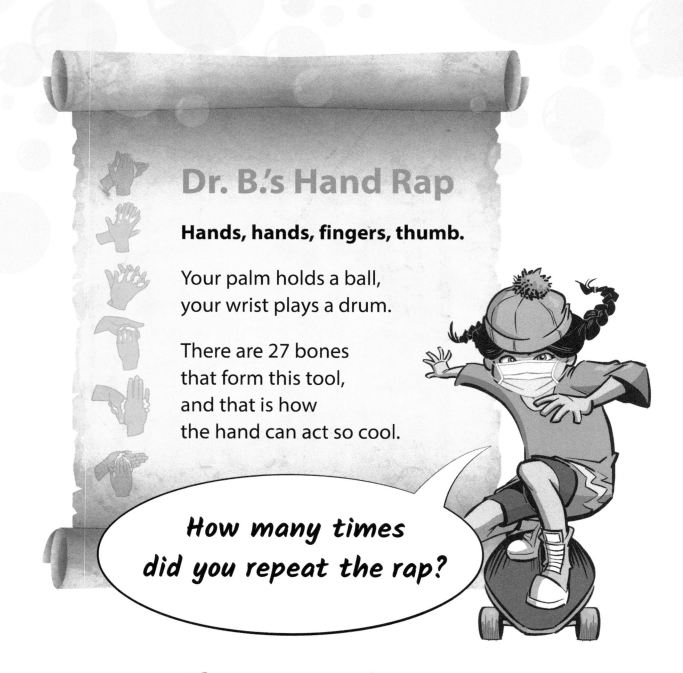

Dr. B.'s Hand Rap

Hands, hands, fingers, thumb.

Your palm holds a ball,
your wrist plays a drum.

There are 27 bones
that form this tool,
and that is how
the hand can act so cool.

**How many times
did you repeat the rap?**

**If you counted,
what number did you get up to?**

This is how long you should wash your hands every time you wash them!

You can kill pesky germs even if you are not close to a sink
by using hand sanitizer. Protect yourself from germs and viruses
by keeping your hands clean. It's easy.

Hugs Not Bugs

From infancy, touch is tied deeply to our emotions. All ages need and use the sense of touch, from young to old, between friends and family, classmates and teammates.

A **handshake**, **hug**, or a **pat on the back** can instill a sense of trust, strengthen relationships, and increase cooperation.

People usually hug their friends and families to express love. But did you know that beyond that warm and fuzzy feeling it gives, a hug can actually strengthen your immune system's ability to fight off germs?

When you hug someone, your body releases oxytocin and serotonin, which are both natural mood-elevating hormones. Hormones are chemical messengers that help your organs communicate and tell them to stop or start all kinds of processes, including the creation of white blood cells.

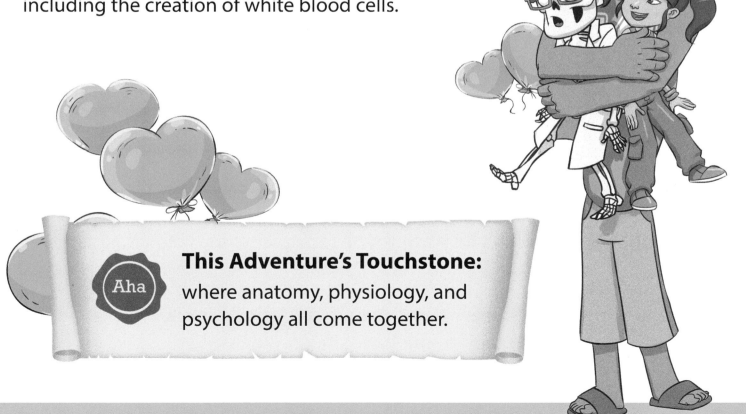

This Adventure's Touchstone: where anatomy, physiology, and psychology all come together.

Aha

Embraceable You!

Try it out!

Find one of your favorite stuffed animals and give it a big squeeze.

How do you feel after?

You connect with another person through hugging, and the feedback helps increase the hormones that make your nervous system feel safe, decreasing hormones that cause stress. Look at the other ways touch has a positive effect:

- **Massage** reduces pain and muscle tension.

- **Petting** a dog or cat lowers blood pressure. Dogs and other animals are often used in therapy.

- **Self-care** when you are stressed or frustrated. You might rub your forehead or hands, flip your hair, or hold your head. You might even hug yourself.

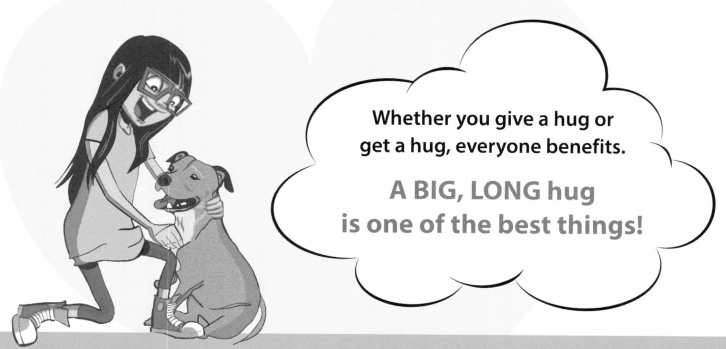

Whether you give a hug or get a hug, everyone benefits.

A BIG, LONG hug is one of the best things!

Fever Believer

You might already know that your body gets colder in the winter and hotter in the summer, but did you know that your temperature can change depending on what's going on inside you?

Your body's temperature changes throughout the day depending on what you're doing.

For example, playing and exercising can increase your temperature.

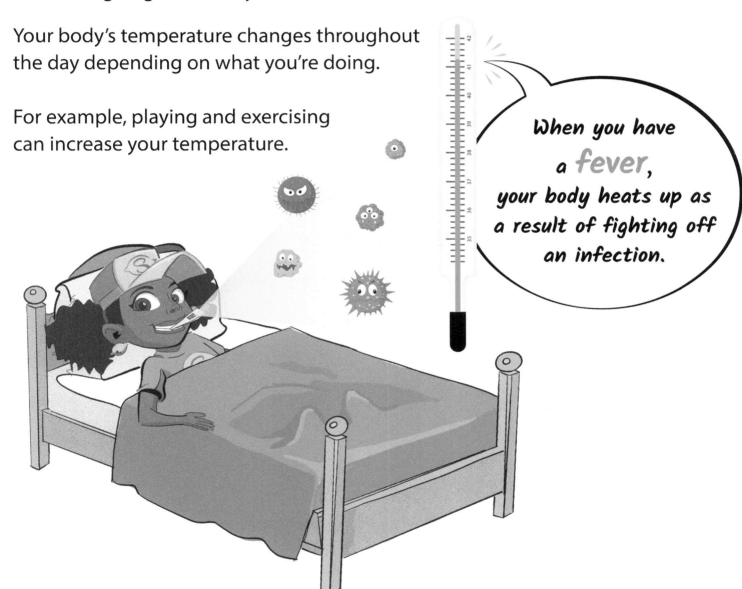

When you have a *fever*, your body heats up as a result of fighting off an infection.

Your parents or doctor generally use a thermometer to check your temperature. A healthy temperature ranges from **97.8** to **99 degrees F (36.5 to 37.2 C)**, though most people have a "normal" resting temperature of 98.6 F (37 C).

Materials:

• **Thermometer**

Directions:

1. Check your temperature with a thermometer.

2. Record results at three different times of the day, at least once after you have been physically active.

3. Record your temperature range below.

What do you observe?

Time	Temperature	Physically Active		
		Low	Med	High
_____	_____	_____	_____	_____
_____	_____	_____	_____	_____
_____	_____	_____	_____	_____
_____	_____			

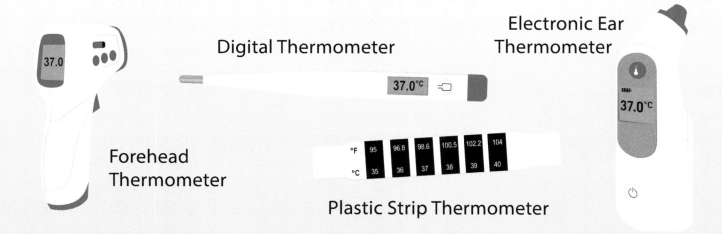

Forehead Thermometer

Digital Thermometer

Electronic Ear Thermometer

Plastic Strip Thermometer

Immune System Word Search

Wild Knights

IMMUNE SYSTEM

MACROPHAGES

LEUKOCYTES

CAMELOT

ENGLAND

LYMPHOCYTES

MIDDLE AGES

HORMONES

KNIGHTS

VIRUS

CALLIGRAPHY

KING ARTHUR

BACTERIA

TCELLS

NEUTROPHILS

MICROBIOME

HYGIENE

BCELLS

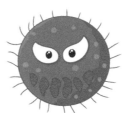
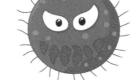

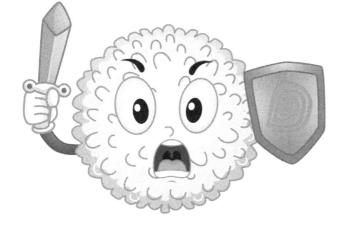

*Answer Keys on page 115.

```
X C D Z O R C B R K I N G A R T H U R S Z M F N X
N L C X W T C T O P I I I B D I Q F D M A X J D U
F C Y A G C M M C E L O U G S N T X E B S Q B E U
Q H L K M M U A I M S E G G W V E U Z T C B D H H
L L J Q X E I Y C D P F U G G M X D K X E N J C S
K A K V O L L C H R D I M K H J A Z K M E O V N H
W M D S T E I O R W O L M P O R V W B D N L W K G
N K H K M L E G T O B P E M U C N F X Y G T H S L
X A T D O X K S S G B A H A U D Y S C W L B O K R
N G P K N I G H T S H I C A G N U T U P A J R J Q
V E S K K B Z P X Q T W O Y G E E K E Y N H M H G
I E U G T I A P T B P V V M X E S S O S D N O L O
R N L T H C V C P G S X F C E O S W Y V M C N K I
U C Y S R V E L T D G B Q T C B Z Z I S T P E O W
S Z M B H O W L K E W L S Q A C M G V E T T S T A
M P P G Y W P I L L R T Y O L E A K M R O E Y Q F
D H H C P C Q H O S X I Q K L L P G F P U B M W F
Z H O H J D H O I A M A A N I L E U I Y N V K G H
I I C G X U U G S L Z P Z X G S Y A K A Q S W H H
L X Y B X D D U Q W S B B B R Y N H Y G I E N E Z
L B T G M Z S L G A D M W O A N V N G V G F H Q U
B N E W J P H Z F P Q H A W P J D X Z K C E V V W
Q S S V L G Y I L L S Q P A H H J E O N P I H M V
I Q Y M W K W W L V Q Q R X Y N T G G C A H A X V
H Y L F O U J I H Z V R W Y R P A T D X P L G L N
```

Bolster Your Defenses

Now that you're armed with knowledge about the immune system, show what you know by filling in the blanks below:

The immune system is made of cells, tissues, and organs that work together

to protect you from i__ __ __ __ __ __ __ __ .

When invaders like b__ __ __ __ __ __ __ or v__ __ __ __ attack your body,

w__ __ __ __ b__ __ __ __ c__ __ __ __ coordinate to detect, devour, and

destroy pathogens. These cells are also known as l__ __ __ __ __ __ __ __ __ ,

and are produced by s__ __ __ c__ __ __ __ in

your b__ __ __ m__ __ __ __ __ .

The two types of leukocytes are l__ __ __ __ __ __ __ __ __ __ __ , whose job

is to 'remember and recognize' invaders, and p__ __ __ __ __ __ __ __ __ ,

which are responsible for 'eating up' pathogens. Within these types,

different cells have even more specific roles.

Lymphocyte types are __ cells, which help attack invaders, and __ cells, which

make a__ __ __ __ __ __ __ __ __ ; these identify and neutralize pathogens.

Phagocyte types include m_ _ _ _ _ _ _ _ _ ,

n_ _ _ _ _ _ _ _ _ _ , and e_ _ _ _ _ _ _ _ _ _ .

The biggest group of all white blood cells, n_ _ _ _ _ _ _ _ _ _ ,

move around your blood looking for antigens. The largest of all white

blood cells, m_ _ _ _ _ _ _ _ _ _ , live in different parts of

your body and are responsible for detecting and destroying invaders.

E_ _ _ _ _ _ _ _ _ _ direct cell movements.

The immune system labels cells with a 'uniform', called a h_ _ _ _

l_ _ _ _ _ _ _ _ _ a_ _ _ _ _ _ . This 'uniform' helps the immune

system identify cells. When it recognizes the uniform, it does not attack.

Even when it's not battling invaders, your immune system is on duty keeping

you healthy. A system of 'good' bacteria lives in your colon, called the

m_ _ _ _ _ _ _ _ _ . This system helps support and strengthen

your immunity. Everyone's microbiome is unique; depending on your age

and environment, there are between _ _ _ and _ _ _ _ different kinds

of bacteria living in your gut.

✳ Answer Keys on page 116.

Experience Foods from Arthurian England

The tales of Arthurian England were set in early medieval times (between the fall of the Roman Empire around the fifth century BCE and the Renaissance around the fourteenth century BCE), when most people in England had difficult lives. They had to fight off invaders from all sides, and even in peaceful times, they lived in villages and on farms where they worked hard to raise a few basic, staple foods.

Although fish and milk were part of their diet, villagers relied on grains, vegetables, and herbs. These ingredients were combined into a stew called "pottage" to make them last longer. Only the richest people could afford meat and bread.

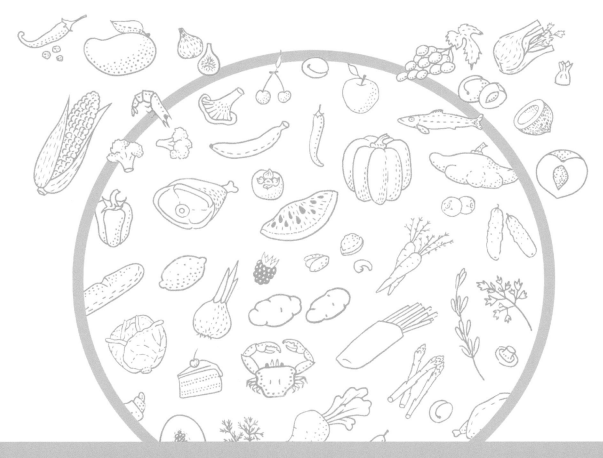

Pinky's Hint:

Read through the entire recipe before beginning to prepare food. This way, you'll know what equipment and ingredients are needed, and you'll be familiar with the steps involved.

 Whenever you see the chef's hat icon, it means **you'll need an adult's help**.

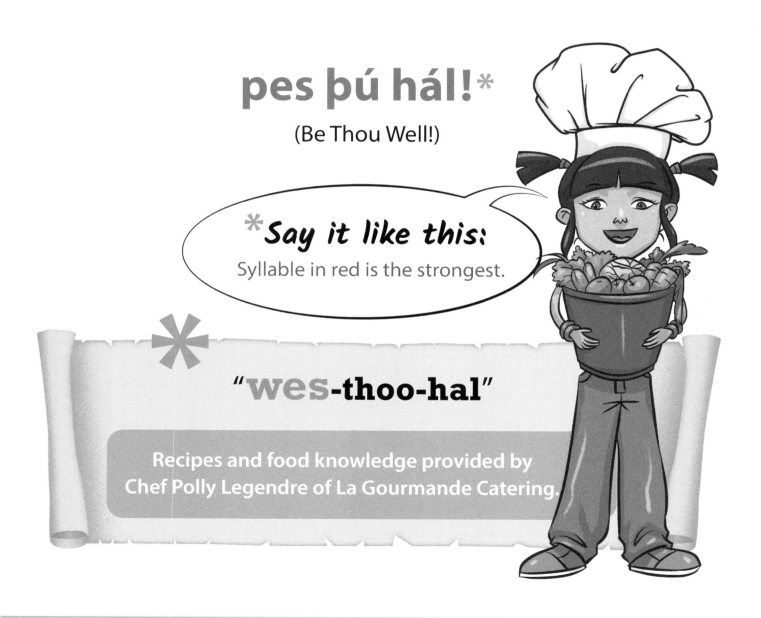

pes þú hál!*

(Be Thou Well!)

*Say it like this:
Syllable in red is the strongest.

*

"**wes**-thoo-hal"

Recipes and food knowledge provided by Chef Polly Legendre of La Gourmande Catering.

Vegetable Pottage

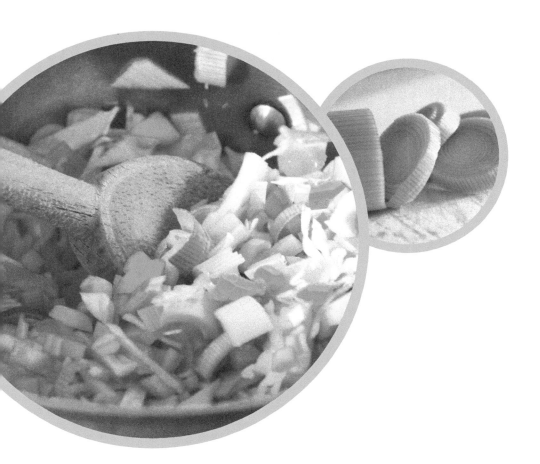

Serves 4

**Total time:
35 minutes**

Ingredients:

- 3 whole leeks, with the dark green leaves removed
- 2 carrots
- 1 onion
- 2 cloves garlic
- 1/4 head of green cabbage
- 3 cups of vegetable or chicken broth
- Salt and pepper to taste

Preparation:

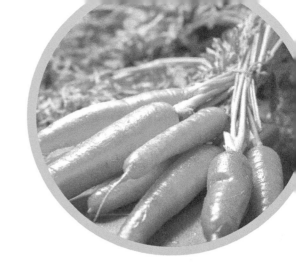

 1. Slice the leeks lengthwise to remove any dirt between the layers; then rinse.

 2. Peel the carrots, onion, and garlic, and chop all the vegetables into small pieces.

 3. Put all the vegetables into a soup pot and pour in the broth.

 4. Bring to a boil over high heat; then reduce to a simmer and cook for about 15 minutes or until the vegetables are all tender.

5. Season with salt and pepper to taste, and serve.

 Show off your cooking skills!

Have your grown up take a photo, and share on social media using the hashtag:

#KnowYourAdventure!

KnowYourselfOAK   KnowYourselfOAK

Baked Apples with Oats

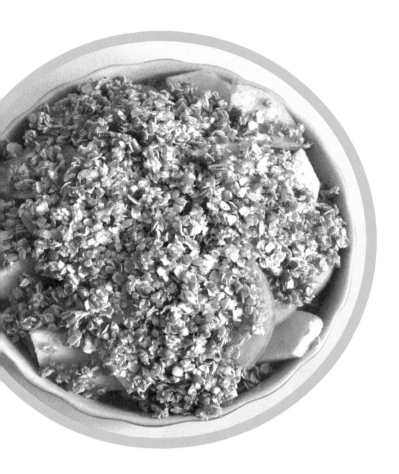

Serves 4

**Total time:
45 minutes**

Ingredients:

- 4 apples
- 1 cup quick rolled oats
- 1/3 cup brown sugar
- 1/3 cup butter
- 1 tsp ground cinnamon

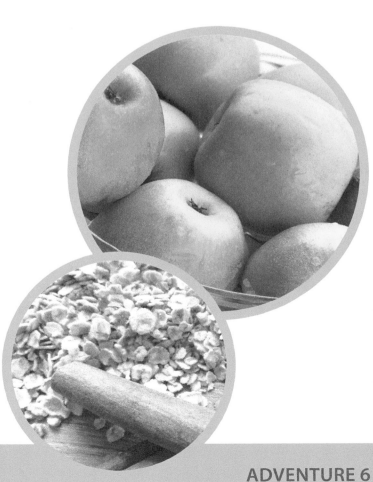

Preparation:

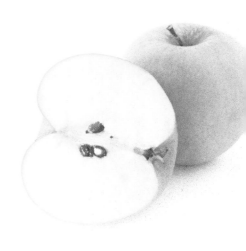

1. Preheat the oven to 350 degrees.

 2. Cut each apple into quarters, and then remove the core.

 3. Slice the apple quarters into thin slices, and put into an ovenproof dish or pan.

4. Mix oats, brown sugar, and cinnamon together in a bowl, and then add in the butter in slowly until evenly combined.

5. Top the apples with the oat mixture, spreading it around to completely cover the apples.

 6. Bake in the preheated oven until apples are tender and topping is golden brown (about 30 minutes).

Dr B.'s Note

A nobleman would never be found eating fresh fruit, as it was considered "peasant food."
For this recipe, you shall consider yourself noble.

Thoughts for Young Chefs

If the foods from England's Dark Ages were all you could eat, which of your favorite foods would you miss the most?

_____

_____

_____

_____

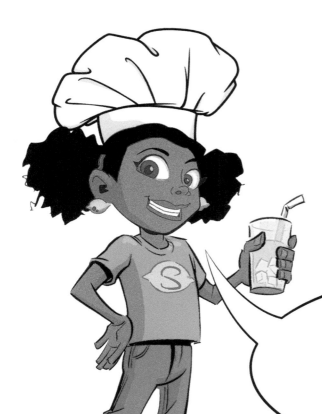

Record and compare the foods you eat **at home** and the foods **in Aurthurian England**.

Write the foods that *are the same* in the shaded area.

Food for thought:

What are the similarities and differences?

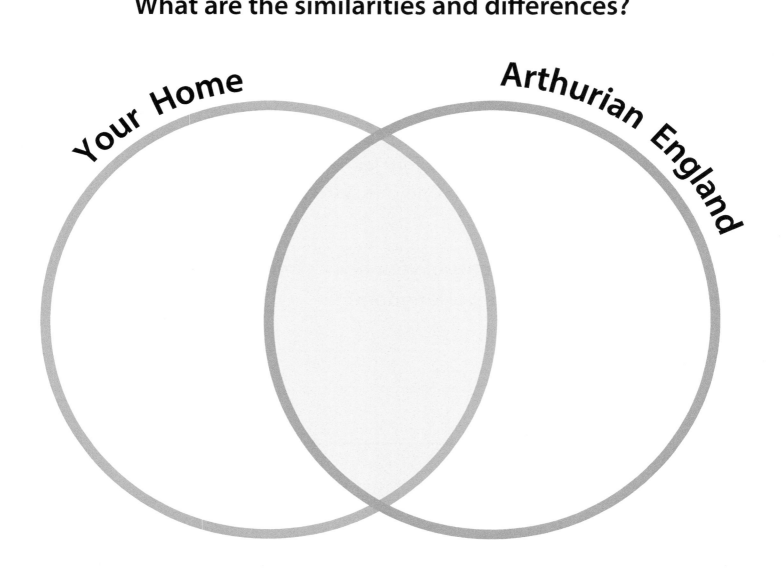

Your Home

Arthurian England

What type of food are you inspired to make next?

_____

_____

_____

Knight School Final Quest

You've done a lot of hard work!

Now that you're nearing the end of your journey, show us what you have learned about Arthurian England and the immune system.

- **How are the components of your body's immune system similar to the knights of a medieval kingdom?**

_____

_____

_____

_____

_____

_____

_____

● What are some ways that life in the Dark Ages would have made it difficult to practice good hygiene?

_____

_____

_____

_____

_____

● What are some important ways that you can practice good hygiene today to keep your family, your community, and yourself safe?

_____

_____

_____

_____

_____

Know Thyself, Young Knight

According to legend, the Knights of the Round Table followed a code of conduct valuing virtues of generosity, courtesy, valour, and fairness, among others. Maybe King Arthur and his Knights of the Round Table didn't exist. Maybe they did. But one thing is for certain: societies develop codes of conduct, written or unwritten, that guide communication, interaction, and governance.

Here is an example of the
Know Yourself Code of Chivalry,
organized by virtue.

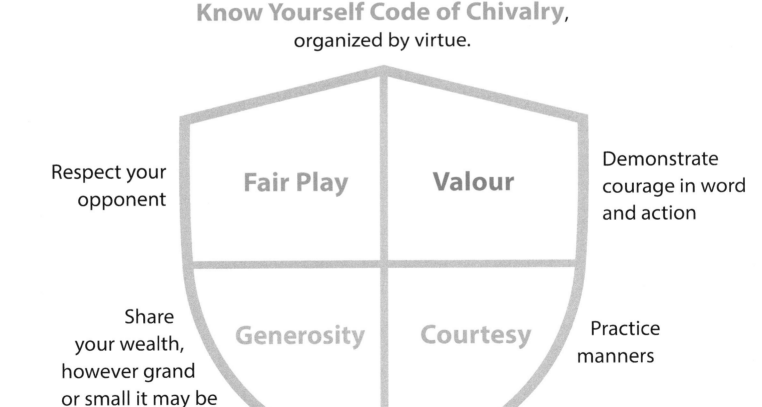

Respect your opponent — **Fair Play**

Valour — Demonstrate courage in word and action

Share your wealth, however grand or small it may be — **Generosity**

Courtesy — Practice manners

How many days can you practice the Know Thyself Code of Chivalry?

No one's perfect! Can you practice some of them every day for a week?

All of them?

	Fair Play	Valour	Generosity	Courtesy
sample	✔			✔
MON				
TUES				
WEDS				
THURS				
FRI				
SAT				
SUN				

DIY Hand Sanitizer

The best way to protect yourself from infection and to avoid spreading germs to others is **to wash your hands correctly and frequently**.

If you do not have soap and water available, you should use a hand sanitizer or hand rub to kill the germs that may be on your hands. If you cannot find hand sanitizer at the store, World Health Organization has recommended a formulation you can make at home as a last resort.

You can find information and instructions:

www.who.int/gpsc/5may/Guide_to_Local_Production.pdf

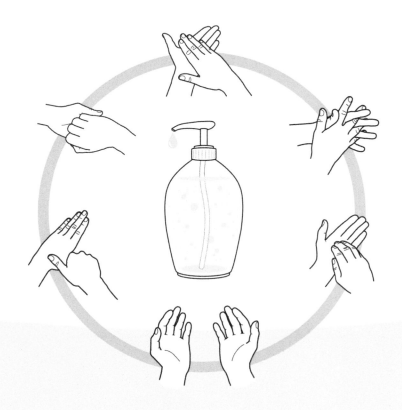

Face Mask

Wearing a face mask is a very important way to limit the spread of germs between people. If we all wear our own, we can help keep our communities healthy.

Have you bought or made one yet?

If not, you can visit the Know Yourself website to learn about the opportunities to win or buy one through us.

You can also follow in the next page the instructions for the Centers for Disease Control and Prevention's (CDC) recommendations on making a mask at home.

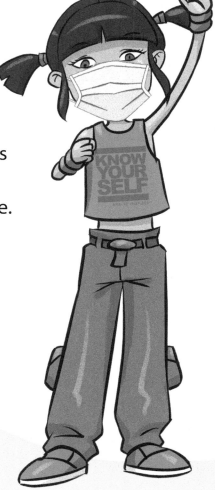

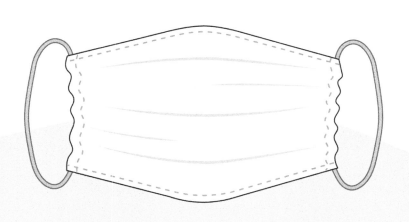

Sewn Mask

Materials:

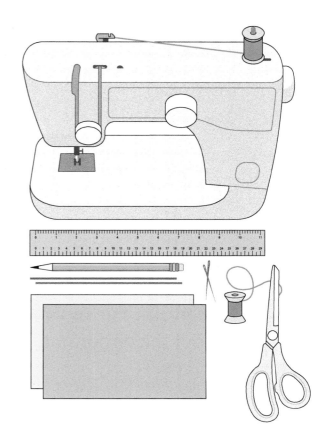

- **Two 10"x6" rectangles of cotton fabric**

- **Two 6" pieces of elastic (or rubber bands, string, cloth strips, or hair ties)**

- **Needle and thread (or bobby pin)**

- **Scissors**

- **Sewing machine**

Directions:

1. Cut out two 10 by 6-inch rectangles of cotton fabric. Use tightly woven cotton, such as quilting fabric or cotton sheets. T-shirt fabric will work in a pinch. Stack the two rectangles; you will sew the mask as if it was a single piece of fabric.

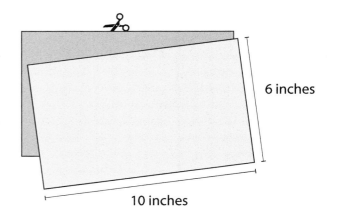

6 inches

10 inches

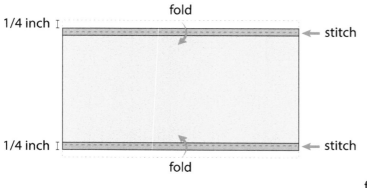

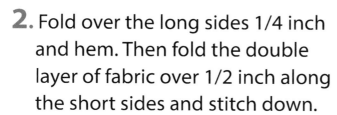

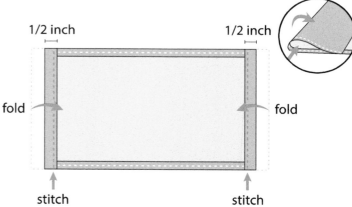

2. Fold over the long sides 1/4 inch and hem. Then fold the double layer of fabric over 1/2 inch along the short sides and stitch down.

3. Run a 6-inch length of 1/8-inch wide elastic through the wider hem on each side of the mask. These will be the ear loops. Use a large needle or a bobby pin to thread it through.

Tie the ends tight. Don't have elastic? Use hair ties or elastic head bands. If you only have string, you can make the ties longer and tie the mask behind your head.

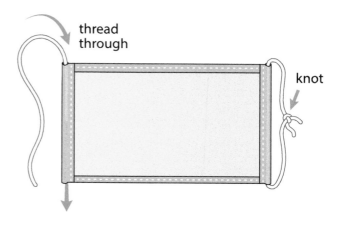

4. Gently pull on the elastic so that the knots are tucked inside the hem. Gather the sides of the mask on the elastic and adjust so the mask fits your face. Then securely stitch the elastic in place to keep it from slipping.

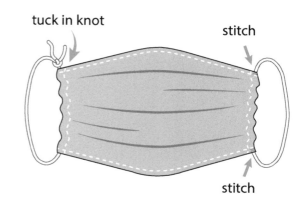

Quick Cut T-shirt Face Covering

(no sew method)

Materials:

- **Old T-shirt** • **Scissors**

Directions:

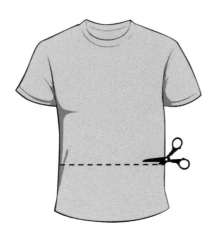

1. Cut 7-8 inches off the bottom of an old T-shirt.

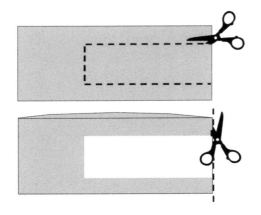

2. Cut 6-7 inches into the middle of the material to make tie strings.

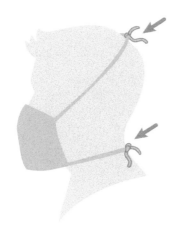

3. Tie strings around neck, then over top of head.

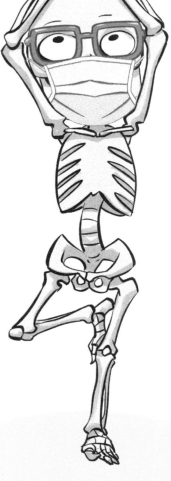

Bandana Face Covering
(no sew method)

Materials:

- **Bandana** (or square cotton cloth approximately 20" x 20")

- **Or an old silk scarf** is great

- **Rubber bands** (or hair ties)

- **Scissors** (if you are cutting your own cloth)

Directions:

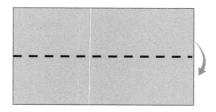

1. Fold bandana in half.

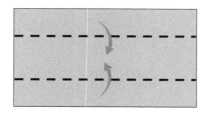

2. Fold top down, fold bottom up.

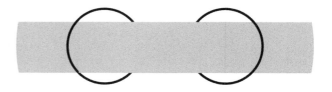

3. Place rubber bands or hair ties about 6 inches apart.

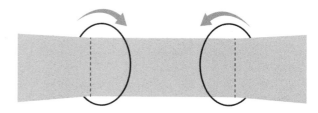

4. Fold side to the middle and tuck.

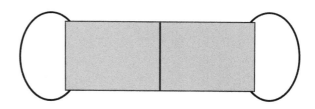

5. Completed.

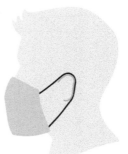

6. Place bandana ties around ears.

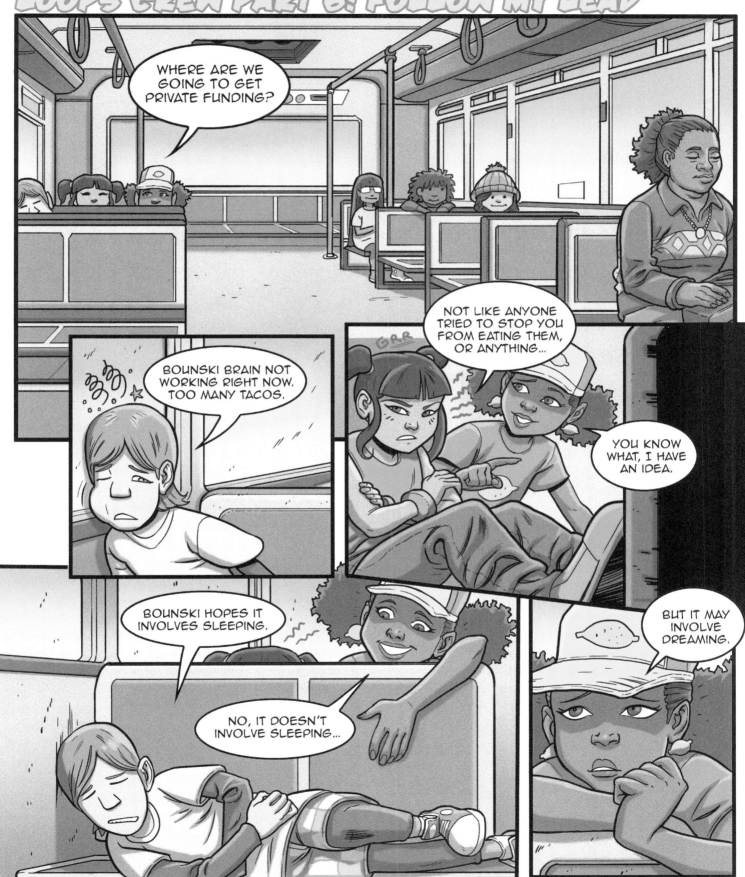

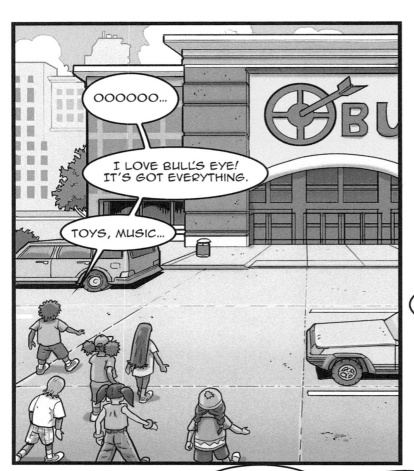
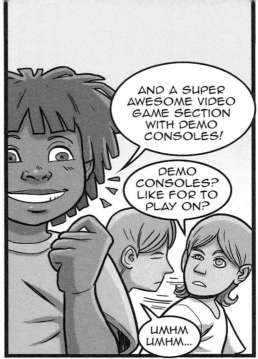
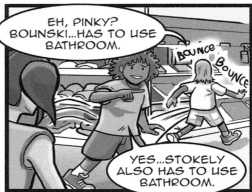
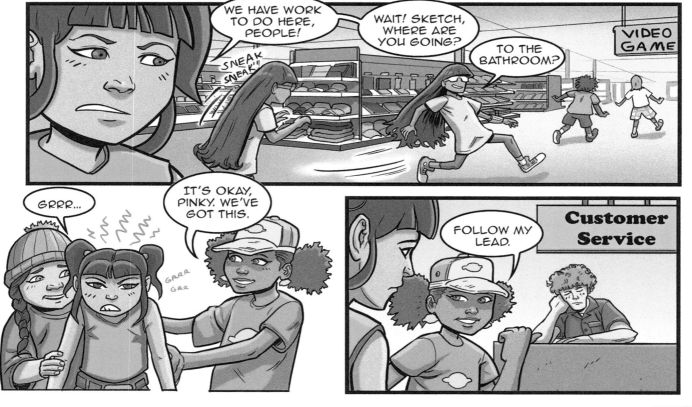

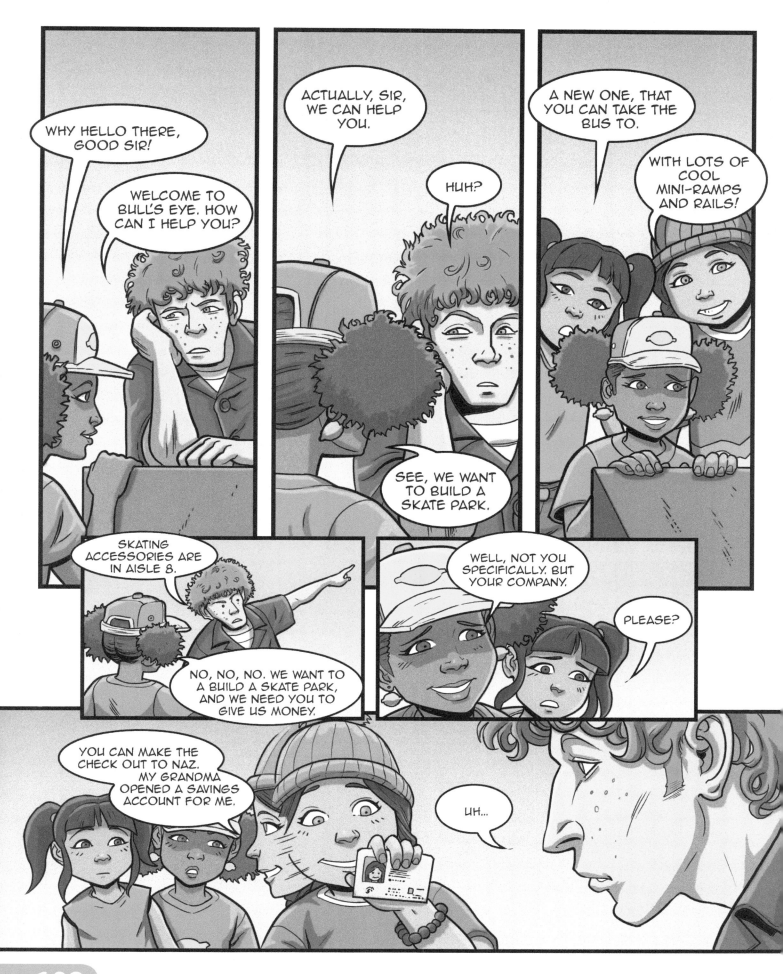

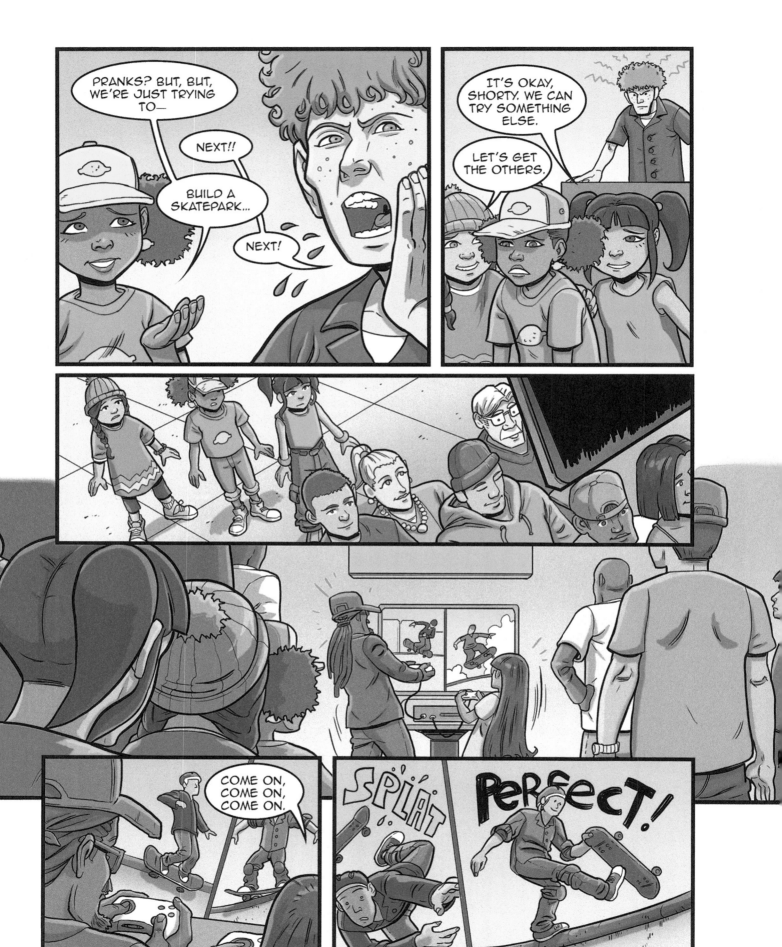

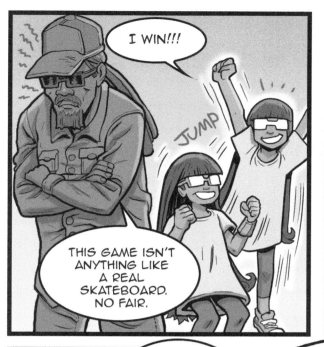

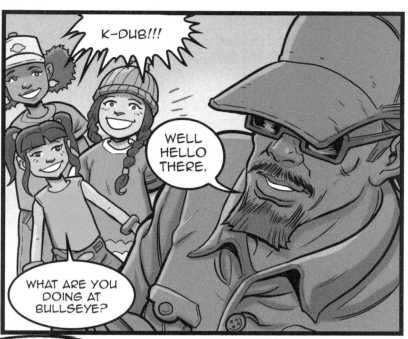

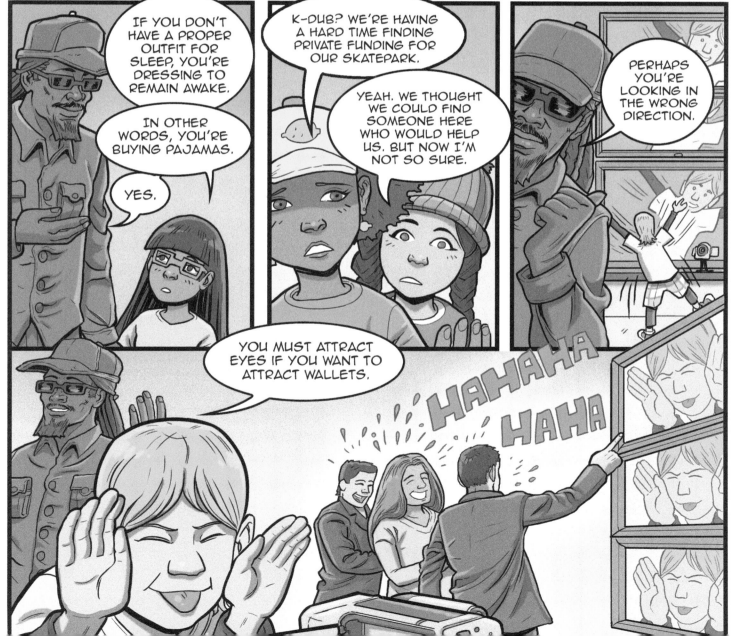

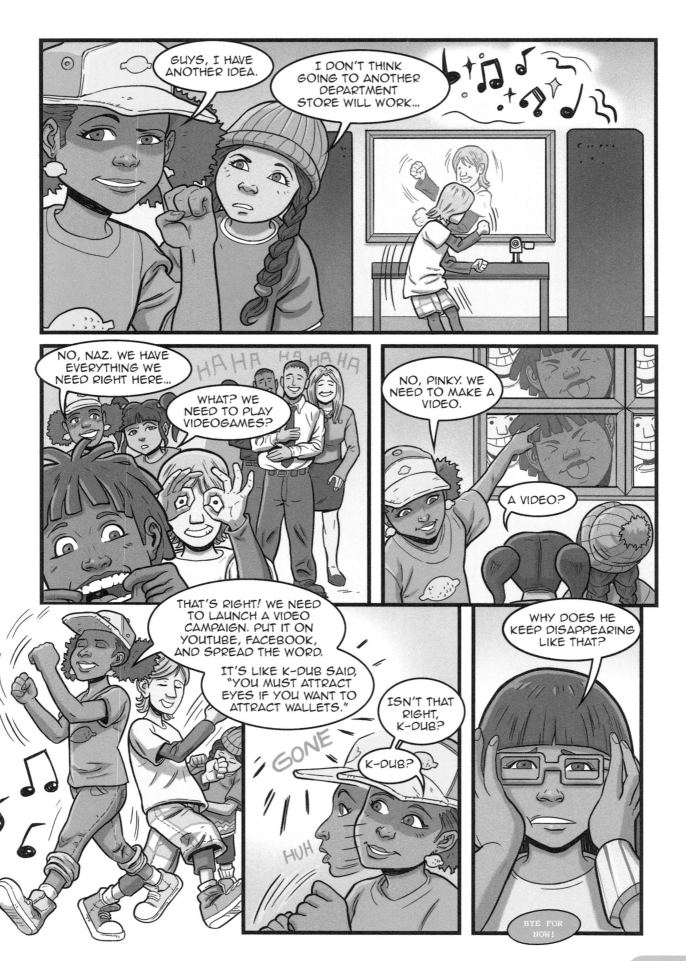

The Muscular System

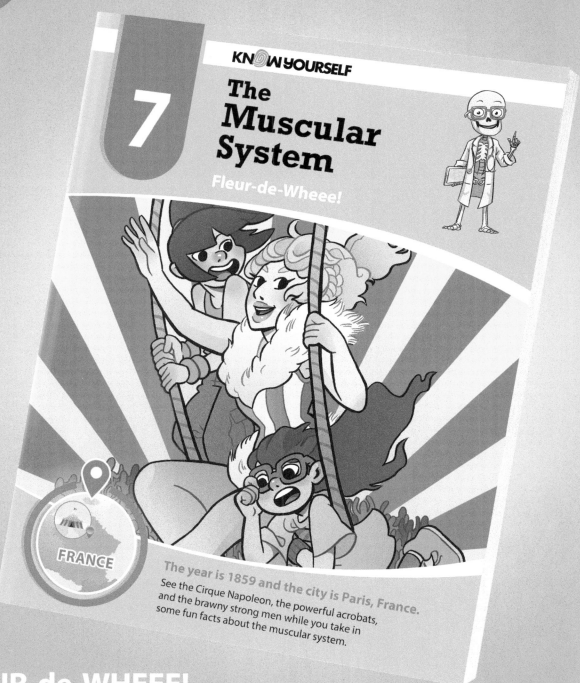

KNOW YOURSELF

7 The Muscular System

Fleur-de-Wheee!

FRANCE

The year is 1859 and the city is Paris, France. See the Cirque Napoleon, the powerful acrobats, and the brawny strong men while you take in some fun facts about the muscular system.

FLEUR-de-WHEEE!

The year is 1859 and the city is Paris, France.

See the Cirque Napoleon, the powerful acrobats, and the brawny strong men while you take in some fun facts about the muscular system.